P9-DOF-619

GUSTAVO GUTIÉRREZ

MAKERS OF CONTEMPORARY THEOLOGY

GUSTAVO GUTIÉRREZ

by

ROBERT McAFEE BROWN

John Knox Press
ATLANTA

Scripture quotations are from the Revised Standard Version Bible, copyright 1946, 1952 and © 1971, 1973 by the Division of Christian Education of the National Council of the Churches of Christ in the U. S. A. and are used by permission.

Library of Congress Cataloging in Publication Data

Brown, Robert McAfee, 1920–
   Gustavo Gutiérrez.

   (Makers of contemporary theology)
   Bibliography: p.
   1. Gutiérrez, Gustavo, 1928–
BX4705.G786B76   261.8   80–82185
ISBN 0–8042–0651–1 (pbk.)

Acknowledgement is made for permission to quote from the following:
National Catholic Reporter: "Gustavo Gutiérrez," by Agostin Bono, in *National Catholic Reporter*, 15 February 1974.
Orbis Books: "Introduction," by Gustavo Gutiérrez, in *Between Honesty and Hope*, edited by Peruvian Bishops' Commission for Social Action; *A Theology of Liberation: History, Politics, and Salvation*, by Gustavo Gutiérrez; "Statement by Gustavo Gutiérrez," by Gustavo Gutiérrez, and "Statement by José Míguez Bonino," by José Míguez Bonino, in *Theology in the Americas*, edited by Sergio Torres and John Eagleson; and "Two Theological Perspectives: Liberation Theology and Progressivist Theology," by Gustavo Gutiérrez, in *The Emergent Gospel: Theology from the Underside of History*, edited by Sergio Torres and Virginia Fabella.
Seabury Press: "Liberation, Theology and Practice," by Gustavo Gutiérrez, in *The Mystical and Political Dimension of the Christian Faith*, Concilium Series No. 96, edited by Claude Geffré and Gustavo Gutiérrez; and "The Poor in the Church," by Gustavo Gutiérrez, in *The Poor and the Church*, Concilium Series No. 104, edited by Norbert Greinacher and Alois Müller.
The Witness: "Terrorism, Liberation, and Sexuality," and "Where Hunger Is, God Is Not," by Gustavo Gutiérrez, in *The Witness*, April 1977.

[Gutiérrez' language is] language on the homiletic rather than the theological level. We are hearing a Christian, not a theologian, speaking.
  —Alfredo Fierro[1]

Is better to be Christian than theologian.
  —Gustavo Gutiérrez, in conversation.

All the political theologies, the theologies of hope, of revolution, and of liberation, are not worth one act of genuine solidarity with exploited social classes. They are not worth one act of faith, love, and hope, committed—in one way or another—in active participation to liberate persons from everything that dehumanizes them and prevents them from living according to the will of God.
  —Gustavo Gutiérrez[2]

* * * * * * *

[Liberation theology] does not answer only the questions, What is to be believed? and What is to be said? It wants to answer the question, What is to be done?
  —Claude Geffré[3]

Table of Contents

Arranging the Program Notes

A drama is being staged in the world today. Whether it will be a comedy or a tragedy remains to be seen. Everybody is an actor in the drama (including all the readers of this book) but not everybody knows it (including some of the readers of this book). The stakes are high.

The initiators of the drama are the ones Frantz Fanon has called "the wretched of the earth." They have learned that they do not need to remain wretched. God did not ordain wretchedness for them, despite what some of God's emissaries have told them. There are goods enough to go around, but the rich have most of them. The poor are demanding their fair share of those goods. The rich are not willing to comply.

Those are the components of the drama. It is a struggle for life. The alternative is death. The stakes are high indeed.

The struggle is increasingly referred to as the liberation struggle. It is initiated by victims of oppression who want liberation, not as a theoretical concept, but as a condition of physical survival and full humanity.

The churches have a long track record of opposing liberation struggles. They have tended to side with the upholders of the *status quo* who are the enemies of liberation, those whom the oppressed call the oppressors.

But in a few parts of the world, the churches—or at least certain people within the churches—have deliberately entered the drama on the side of those seeking liberation. Where this has happened, notably in Latin America, a theology has emerged that is called, appropriately enough, a theology of liberation.

This book is a brief introduction to the theology of liberation as it has been developed by one of its chief exponents, Gustavo Gutiérrez.

Or, alternately, one could say: this book is a brief introduction to the theology of Gustavo Gutiérrez, as it has been developed by him in the form of a theology of liberation. The two go hand-in-glove, as we shall discover in the first two chapters. But he has been liberation theology's servant rather than its creator or master. And today it is from the servants rather than the masters that we are most likely to learn.

The introduction is a partisan one. I make no apologies for that. In the liberation struggle there is no neutrality. Not to be for the liberation of oppressed peoples is to contribute, by default, to their continuing oppression. So I believe we must take sides in the drama that is being waged. I have discovered, through exposure to liberation theology and liberation theologians, that with the best will in the world I and people like me are often on the wrong side. In the imagery of that paradigm of liberation stories—the exodus from Egypt—we turn out to be servants in Pharaoh's court rather than subversive agents working for the liberation of the slaves. This is, at best, an uncomfortable discovery, and part of what this book should do is to spread the discomfort around in more wholesale fashion. Discomfort is not the last word of the gospel. But it may be an important first word to hear before we are entitled to hear the last word, which for us, too, in however different an accent, is the good news of liberation.

I believe that Gustavo Gutiérrez has restated the gospel in a compelling, if disquieting, way. In the following pages we will seek to become acquainted with him and his situation; then we will try to hear what he says, on his own terms and for his own situation; after that we will listen briefly to what the critics say; and finally, we will face the question of what it means for us.

So that he can be heard on "his own terms," there are frequent quotations from his writings, about which the following should be said:

1. Since Gutiérrez' major work, *A Theology of Liberation*, is easily available, most of the quotations have been taken from other writings, in order to widen our acquaintance with him. Nevertheless, *A Theology of Liberation* is the place to go from here

for fuller exposure. The purpose of writing this book is to make you want to read that one.

2. Sometimes the quotations are slightly modified, to avoid sexist language. This procedure has their author's approval. One result of Gutiérrez' teaching women students has not only been his conscientization of them, but their conscientization of him. Furthermore, nobody should be able to avoid the impact of his thought by retreating into a linguistic cubbyhole.

A personal word. I taught on the same theological faculty with Gustavo Gutiérrez for two semesters. My wife and I got to know him, both in the classroom and in our home, and we later visited him in Lima. Personal encounter with him has been an important reality in my ongoing theological journey—a journey whose direction he has drastically re-routed. For the rest of this book he will be referred to as "Gustavo," not because I want to exploit a personal friendship, but for the simple reason that absolutely everybody who knows him does so. Nothing would be less authentic in writing about this unprepossessing and genuinely humble man than to call him "Professor" or "Father" or "Doctor" or "Gutiérrez." He is Gustavo, plain and simple, to those who know him.

Come along and get to know him, too. . .

CHAPTER ONE

A Collective Biography
of the Authors

All liberation theology originates among the world's
anonymous, whoever may write the books or the declarations articulating it.[4]

Gustavo writes a lot of "the books or the declarations" articulating liberation theology. But it is not his individual creation.
Nor has it arisen out of the university classroom where he teaches
one day each week. It has arisen out of the experiences of the
poor, the oppressed, the "wretched of the earth" in Latin
America, with whom he lives six days each week. "The world's
anonymous," the people, are the real creators of liberation theology, although it is fortunate that Gustavo (along with friends like
Juan Luis Segundo, José Porfirio Miranda, Leonardo Boff, José
Míguez Bonino, Raúl Vidales, and Jon Sobrino) not only shares
their experiences, but puts them down on paper for the rest of us.

So although this is a book about Gustavo, one can only write
about him by writing about the people with whom he lives and
works. To isolate him, to put him in an academic setting, to
depict him as telling people what to think, or even to describe
him as sitting in a library pouring over the writings of earlier
theologians (although he clearly has to do his share of the latter)
would be to falsify the story from the start. He must be positioned in the midst of the people with whom he works and to
whose cause he has committed himself. So we have to widen the
stage at the very beginning to include them, and get enough
historical background to understand them all.

From the earliest invasions of the Spanish *conquistadores*, almost five centuries ago, Latin America has been the object of what is politely called "colonial rule," which less politely means being exploited and dominated by outsiders. Until recently the outsiders were Spaniards and Portuguese; now they are North Americans and northern Europeans. The early invaders treated the Indians ruthlessly, and one bishop, Bartolomé de Las Casas, took the side of the Indians, incurring the wrath of the money-conscious Spaniards who saw exploitation of the Indians as a way to get rich quick. Las Casas is a special hero of Gustavo, as we shall see, and could be called the first liberation theologian, unless we wish to reserve that designation for another special hero of Gustavo, Jesús de Nazaret.

In the nineteenth century there were nationalistic uprisings in Latin America that secured a measure of self-rule. But only a measure, for although overt *political control* from Europe was generally overthrown, covert *economic control* replaced it (a shift from what liberation theologians call "colonialism" to "neo-colonialism"). Economic manipulators abroad joined forces with small indigenous manipulators at home to continue the exploitation of the many by the few.

Since there were not many Bartolomé de Las Casas around, the Catholic Church tended through the centuries to identify with the rich, and to console the poor with promises of reward in an afterlife, provided the poor remained submissive to those whom an all-wise Providence had placed over them. It was a good arrangement for the rich, and also a good arrangement for the church, which became not only the church of the rich, but also a rich church.

This bleak ecclesiastical picture has been changing in recent years. For although the oppression of the poor by the rich has continued, the complicity of the church in this oppression has diminished, and in some quarters turned into outright opposition. There are at least two reasons for this.

One reason has been an increasing unwillingness of priests to be puppets of the rich. A good many became dissatisfied at serving in conventional parishes (administering just enough "charity" to defuse whatever revolutionary zeal the poor might otherwise have developed) and began to identify directly with the poor, sometimes leaving posh parishes to live in the *barrios* or *poblaciones*—what, in less esoteric language, we would call the slums. This represented a literal "conversion" experience, i.e. being "turned around," to identify no longer with the rich but with the poor. As the priests listened to the poor, and as they re-read their Bibles with the poor, they concluded that it was *by* and *for* just such people that the Bible had originally been written. Its clear message was "good news *to the poor*," as Jesus said so well (cf. Luke 4:16–30).

"Good news to the poor" could only initially be bad news to the rich, since those who keep the poor poor are answerable for thwarting, subverting, or denying the good news. More than that, social structures that benefited the rich (such as huge landed estates owned by a minority, widespread acceptance of the practice of paying starvation wages or less, strong anti-union sentiment) continued to destroy the poor. So part of the "good news to the poor" meant opposing such unjust structures. Which meant seeking to overthrow them. Which meant "taking sides." Which meant politics. Which meant revolution. Along such paths were the priests led.

The rich responded that this was dirty pool. The church was "taking sides," and that was no fair. The church was supposed to be above mundane squabbles, preaching eternal verities and salvation in heaven. Not so, responded those captured by the new vision, the church was not suddenly "taking sides," it was only "changing sides." It had always been on the side of the rich, with no noticeable complaints from the rich; now it was going to be on the side of the poor, since that was the mandate of the gospel. What could be fairer than that?

This identification of certain priests and Christians with the poor and oppressed, and a desire to learn from them, did not happen in a vacuum. There was a *second reason* for it, a long history of Catholic "social teaching," through papal encyclicals and other documents, that began to converge in the same direction. The story is too long to tell here, but the substance of the story is that the church gradually inched its way into the modern world, which meant the world of the oppressed.[5] Beginning in 1891, a series of "social encyclicals" appeared over eighty years, in which the church's official teaching about political engagement underwent slow but startling change. Early on, there were routine condemnations of "atheistic communism," and criticism of Catholics who were soft on socialism. But the tone changed as it became clearer that workers in the modern world had a right to organize, to strike, to insist on a decent standard of living, and to assume more control over their lives—things that the economic and political system known as "capitalism" had a deeply ingrained habit of opposing, and did not propose to concede without a fight. But by the time of Paul VI's apostolic letter, *Octogesima Adveniens* (1971), it was acknowledged that socialism was an option Catholics could entertain, so long as they observed certain safeguards.

The Second Vatican Council, meeting in Rome from 1961 to 1965, opened new doors to the modern world, and (without coming out and espousing socialism) affirmed the new currents that had been emerging, an example of listening to "the voice of God" as found in "the voice of the times." Since the most clamorous "voice of the times" was the cry of the poor, the stage was set for Latin American bishops to consider what all this said to their continent, and to move beyond the carefully modulated pronouncements of Vatican II. They gathered to do so in 1968 in Medellín, Colombia. Their topic was "The Church in the Present-Day Transformation of Latin America in the Light of the Council."

By any reckoning Medellín was a landmark for both the Latin American and the world church. The bishops issued a series of sixteen documents, and at least three of them were very good indeed—which is a high batting average for corporate episcopal prose. The text of the most important, the one on "Peace," was basically the work of a single priest who did the actual writing for the bishops dealing with that subject. The priest was Gustavo. The document insisted that violence does not begin only when a gun is fired, but is already present in the "structural violence" that condemns the great majority of Latin Americans to poverty, hunger, despair, and death. The true "violence" is found in structures so rigged that benefits for the few are purchased at the cost of destruction for the many. It was because of such documents that Medellín is known as the conference at which the church opted positively for the oppressed, attacked the political and economic structures of Latin America as purveyors of injustice, pointed out the unjust dependency of Latin America on outside powers, and called for radical change across the continent. Medellín saw clearly that the present order of things guarantees that the rich will grow richer at the expense of the poor, with the inevitable result that the poor will grow poorer in relation to the rich. And the bishops refused any longer to bless such an order of things. Strong stuff.

Two further realities, present in a small way before Medellín, grew much stronger after Medellín.

One reality was the extraordinary growth of the *communidades de base*, base communities, or, as we might better say, "grassroots communities." There may now be as many as one hundred thousand of these in Latin America: Brazil alone claims eighty thousand. They are small groups of persons, perhaps fifteen to twenty, who gather to deal with a variety of local problems, often with a priest, sometimes without. They share a liturgical life, engage in Bible study, and tackle situations of injustice, from the unwillingness of the local *patrón* to pipe water into "his" village, to concerted action on behalf of political prisoners being subjected to torture. They have become the lifeblood of the Latin American church.

They have become so powerful, in fact, that when the bishops decided to hold a follow-up to Medellín ten years later (finally convened in Puebla, Mexico, in early 1979), the preliminary documents, circulated by the conservative leaders trying to dampen down such unseemly activity, were rousingly attacked all over Latin America. When certain delegates at the conference tried to clip the wings of the *communidades* anyway, they failed. At Puebla, the *communidades* gained stronger episcopal support than they had before.

The second reality that grew stronger after Medellín was liberation theology. For our discussion, the important thing is that the *communidades de base* created liberation theology, not the other way around. Theologians like Gustavo did not muse, "Here are all these new centers of church life, let us provide them with a theology." The reverse was true: as people wrestled with their own problems in the light of their faith, a new way of *doing* theology emerged—not theology from the top down, but from the bottom up, from particular groups of people to all the rest of the people, with Gustavo and others helping to pull it all together so that it could be shared more widely.

So liberation theology is partly a product of Medellín, though foreshadowings of it were present before Medellín. But it is best understood as coming to Medellín and going from it by way of the *communidades de base* out of whose ongoing experience it continues to be refined. The ten years in the Latin American church after Medellín were the decade of the *communidades de base* and their increasing contribution to an understanding of liberation theology.

On both scores, conservative church leaders in Latin America and Rome got nervous. A funny thing was happening to the church on its way to the people, and the leaders were not amused. So in preparation for the Puebla meetings, conservative leaders decided that none of the so-called "liberation theologians" would be invited to work officially with the bishops, even though many of them had done so at Medellín. A scenario was prepared in which liberation theology would be cast aside (or co-opted by a "spiritualized" version), and the *communidades de base* would be so restricted that things could once again be like they were before.

But things are never "once again like they were before," and the scenario failed. The *communidades*, as we have already seen, were resoundingly affirmed, and the condemnations of liberation theology never materialized. The conference, far from downplaying concern for the poor, explicitly affirmed "a preferential option for the poor" as the needed direction for the church in the next decade. The major document proposing this decision was written by Gustavo, who, although officially barred from the meetings, had "friendly bishops" who were willing to present in their own names what he had written for them.

So the poor were heard at Puebla, thanks to Gustavo and the friendly bishops, along with some help from the Holy Spirit. If the rest of the bishops are faithful to the promises they signed at Puebla, the post-Puebla church will increasingly become the church of the poor. It might even become a poor church.

In retrospect, we can see some important steps in the collective biography of the authors of liberation theology. The titles of three volumes of primary source materials (for each of which Gustavo has written an interpretive introduction) capture the moods and attitudes of the last decade: from *Signs of Renewal* (just after Medellín, which was an act of "renewal"), to *Signs of Liberation* (as "renewal" led inexorably to the deeper analysis issuing in liberation movements), to *Signs of Struggle and Hope* (as the realities of liberation engagement took their human toll and yet did not leave their proponents despairing).[6]

Part of Gustavo's interpretation of the Latin American struggle has been an insistence on *the reality of hope* despite—or better, within—the grimness of struggle. To the outsider "grimness" often seems the only way to describe the situation. But for Gustavo that is inadequate. "Oppression, suffering, struggle, those we have always had," he says in conversation. "They are nothing new. They are still with us and will remain with us for a long time. What is new, what is hopeful, is *the awakening of the people* to new possibilities, to taking their future in their own hands. That has been with us only a short time. That is why we can be hopeful. There are always signs of hope within our struggle." In the words of the Peruvian novelist, José Maria Arguedas, whom Gustavo frequently quotes, "What we know is much less than the great hope that we feel."

"The people," who have embodied the "signs of struggle and hope" are the real creators of liberation theology. But they have gotten necessary assistance from "one of the people," Gustavo, and it is time to make his acquaintance.

CHAPTER TWO

An Individual Biography of One Author

Gustavo Gutiérrez has lucidly described his own experience recounting how, from the common Christian and Catholic injunction to help the poor, he was led to understand Christian commitment as solidarity with the struggle of the poor for their liberation.

—Míguez Bonino[7]

In United States I am called theologian. In Peru I am activist.

—Gustavo, in conversation

By northern hemisphere standards, biographical information is easy to report. Within a few lines we can assemble the important "facts" about a person: birth, education, professional appointments, publications, membership in organizations, honors received. *Who's Who* is a model of such compact reporting. On that style, Gustavo can be described as follows:

born June 8, 1928, Lima, Peru;

studied medicine, San Marcos University, Lima, and philosophy, Catholic University, Lima; one semester theology, Santiago de Chile; master's degree in philosophy and psychology, Catholic University, Louvain (Belgium), 1955 (thesis topic: "The Psychic Conflict in Freud"); degree in theology, faculty of theology, Lyon (France), 1959 (unfinished thesis on "Religious Liberty"); ordained priest, 1959; one semester, Gregorian University, Rome (Italy), 1959–60; honorary doctorate in theology, University of Nijmegen (Holland) 1979;

professor in Department of Theology and Social Sciences, Catholic Pontifical University, Lima; advisor, National Union of Catholic Students; advisor, numerous pastoral and theological reflection groups in Peru; founding member ONIS (Oficina Nacionál de Investigación); theological advisor, CELAM II (second conference of Latin American Bishops), Medellín, Colombia, 1968; member, editorial board, *Concilium*; participant, "Christians for Socialism," Santiago de Chile, 1973; founder, Centro Bartolomé de las Casas, Rimac, Lima;

speaker numerous international gatherings, South America, North America, Europe, Asia, Africa (San Antonio, Cartigny, Montreal, Washington, Accra, Dar es Salaam, Sri Lanka, Maryknoll, etc.); visiting professor, Union Theological Seminary, 1976–77; lecturer, "summer course in theology," Catholic University, Lima;

author: (in English) *A Theology of Liberation* (1973); *Praxis of Liberation and Christian Faith* (1974); (with Richard Shaull) *Liberation and Change* (1977); numerous articles and essays in various symposia; (in Spanish) *Líneas pastorales de la Iglesia en América Latina* (1968); *Teología de la liberación: perspectivas* (1971, subsequently translated into nine languages); *La Fuerza Histórica de los Pobres* (1979) to be translated into English in 1981; extensive, indeed innumerable, articles and essays in journals, symposia, conference reports, etc., etc., etc.

Such a compilation may help us to understand some kinds of lives, but it does not help us understand Gustavo, who must be understood on his own terms and in relation to his own culture, rather than having our criteria of what is "important" imposed on him. So let us try to fill in the important things that happened between all those semi-colons.

While some theologies are born in libraries or studies or seminar rooms, Gustavo's theology has been born in the midst of his sharing in the struggle of oppressed peoples to achieve liberation. Where they come from, what their grievances are, why the received theologies are inadequate for them, all influence the theology that grows out of that ongoing struggle. So to look at Gustavo's life is already to have begun an exposition of his theology, and is the only legitimate entrance to it.

Gustavo is not part of Lima's aristocracy, but is a *mestizo*, i.e. part Indian—a Quechuan—and is thus positioned by birth among the oppressed of his nation. As a boy he contracted a severe

case of osteomylitis that forced him to spend six adolescent years
in bed. The disease left him with a permanent limp, which
impedes rapid physical progress, but had no effect on the light-
ning quality of his mind—a trait clearly evident when he talks in
Spanish or French, and increasingly evident in English as his
command of that language improves.

The years in bed inclined him toward a career in medicine,
and during his undergraduate years he took medical studies in
anticipation of becoming a psychiatrist. Those years also included
political activity on the campus of San Marcos University. But
midstream he decided instead to become a priest, and moved
from the university to the seminary—a difficult but important
change of direction.

Promising young Latin American candidates for ordination
were sent to Europe for graduate study, and Gustavo received im-
peccable theological credentials as a result of studying philosophy,
psychology, and theology at Louvain, Lyon, and Rome—the
theological grand tour. François Houtart, a fellow student at Louvain, recalls Gustavo as an excellent student, not at that time
overly political. Houtart feels that the most formative influence
for all of them was probably the presence of *seminaristas* from
many parts of the world; Gustavo formed friendships with other
Latin Americans he would otherwise never have known, among
them Camilo Torres, a "bourgeois" Colombian who later became
radicalized, joined the guerilla forces, and was killed in combat.

Such associations were not part of the prescribed curriculum
on the theological grand tour, and Gustavo, ordained now to the
priesthood, returned to Lima to teach at the Catholic University,
his "formation" having provided solid historical grounding cou-
pled with the best of the *nouvelle theologie* developed by Yves Con-
gar, Henri de Lubac and Jean Daniélou.

But the concerns of Gustavo's undergraduate student activist
days began to reassert themselves, as he once again confronted,
after an absence of almost a decade, the reality of poverty, hope-
lessness, and misery in the lives of the people of Peru, and the
predictable "professional career" started to go in unpredicted directions.

Not to put too fine a point on it, the results of the theological grand tour simply did not come to grips with South American realities, and the next stage in Gustavo's education consisted of unlearning his previous education, re-reading the history of his continent, re-reading the Bible, re-reading theology, and discovering that re-reading means a re-making—a re-making, as far as possible, of the situation of the poor and dispossessed.

At a conference of liberation theologians at El Escoriál in Spain in 1972, Gustavo shared what this impact did to him. While the personal reminiscence is not included in the published report of the conference (in *Fe Cristiana y Cambio Sociál in América Latina*), José Míguez Bonino, who was present on the occasion, has given a report of Gustavo's comments:

> He said (in summary): I discovered three things. I discovered that *poverty was a destructive thing*, something to be fought against and destroyed, not merely something which was the object of our charity. Secondly, I discovered that *poverty was not accidental*. The fact that these people are poor and not rich is not just a matter of chance, but the result of a structure. . . . Thirdly, I discovered that *poor people were a social class*.
>
> When I discovered that poverty was something to be fought against, that poverty was structural, that poor people were a class [and could organize], it became crystal clear that in order to serve the poor, one had to move into political action.[8]

These three crucial discoveries were given a solid historical foundation by Gustavo's rediscovery of Bartolomé de Las Casas (1474–1566), the Spanish bishop earlier referred to, who, during the period of the *conquistadores*, took the side of the Indians as they were being victimized and murdered by his fellow Spaniards.[9] Las Casas' influence on Gustavo is profound and provides important foreshadowings of liberation theology:

● Las Casas affirms a close link between salvation and social justice, asserting that to the degree that the Spaniards exploit the Indians, their own salvation is jeopardized: "It is impossible for someone to be saved, if he does not observe justice."

● Instead of seeing the Indians as "infidels," Las Casas sees them as "the poor" about whom the gospel speaks. They should not be threatened with death if they do not convert—a necessary warning since the Spaniards felt justified in killing Indians who remained "infidels." In the face of this widespread injustice, Las Casas makes a devastating response: it is better to be "a live Indian, even though infidel," than "a dead Indian, even though Christian."

● He judges the theologies of his opponents by their political consequences: theologies that lead to murder and enslavement invalidate their claim to be Christian.

● His own theological reflection begins with the specific case of exploited Indians, rather than with abstract principles from which "applications" are to be deduced. (Sepúlveda, his chief theological opponent, began with an Aristotelian principle that Indians were "naturally inferior" to whites and could therefore be enslaved.)

● He theologizes out of his own participation in the struggle between the *conquistadores* and the Indians, rather than as an outside spectator who can deal with the fate of Indians in purely intellectual terms.

● In the midst of the Indians' plight, he hears Jesus Christ speaking directly to him: "In the Indies I left behind Jesus Christ, our God, suffering affliction, scourging, and crucifixion, not once but a million times over." It is Las Casas' view, Gustavo concludes, that "in and through the 'scourged Christ of the Indies' Jesus is denouncing exploitation, denying the Christianity of the exploiters, and calling people to understand and heed his gospel message." [10]

Between 1960 and 1968, a number of developments in Gustavo's thought were taking place: a gradual break with the "dominant theology" he had learned in Europe and its replacement by liberation theology, an increasing awareness of the importance of Marx's social analysis, and ongoing reflection on the reality of violence in Latin America. (We will consider each of these in subsequent chapters.) His theology was refined not only by his engagement with "the people," but also by a series of meetings with other theologians, several of which are worth noting.

One of the earliest gatherings of theologians committed to exploring the meaning of the faith specifically for Latin America took place at Petrópolis, Brazil, in 1964. Gustavo asked the group how a new pastoral focus could be given to communicating the Word of God today, re-thinking the question of the salvation of non-believers and re-stating the basic characteristics of the Christian life. His growing dissatisfaction with the church's posture, particularly its timidity, was evident in his presentation, and he raised the specific issue of the relationship of the growing revolutionary struggle in Latin America to the gospel's stress on *kenosis* (self-emptying), as well as calling for further thinking about the gospel's understanding of violence and birth control. Some of these intuitions were gathered up in different form in *Líneas Pastorales de la Iglesia en América Latina* (1968), which contrasted earlier approaches to the pastoral task with the emerging prophetic pastoral obligation.

Further clarification came out of a course given at Montreal in 1967, on "The Church and Poverty," the substance of which is included as the last chapter of *A Theology of Liberation*, and which we will later summarize.

But the year in which Gustavo himself feels that liberation theology came to birth is 1968. The occasion was a conference at Chimbote, Peru, sponsored by ONIS, a group of radical priests Gustavo had earlier helped to organize. Here Gustavo presented the fundamental outlines of what he called for the first time "a theology of liberation." Medellín followed a few months later and a considerable number of liberation insights found their way into the Medellín documents (thanks in no small part to the presence there of Gustavo and other members of ONIS). In 1969, a similar presentation was made at a meeting of SODEPAX (Commission on Society, Development and Peace, jointly sponsored by the World Council of Churches and the Pontifical Commission on Justice and Peace) in Cartigny, Switzerland, and the basic outline of what became *A Theology of Liberation* is included in the report of that meeting. (It is typical of Gustavo's single-mindedness that although the Cartigny conference was convened to explore "a theology of development," he unabashedly presented "a theology of liberation"—a distinction we will clarify in Chapter 3.) A theological symposium at Bogotá in 1970 provided a final go-around for the material before its publication in Spanish the following year—after which the whole world began to hear about liberation theology. The socialist implications of this theology are clear in the final document of the conference of "Christians for Socialism" held in Santiago de Chile in April 1973, another text in which the fine hand of Gustavo is apparent.

In the light of the politics that has emerged out of liberation theology, it is well to underline (as Roberto Oliveros has done in *Teología y Liberación*) that it all began with Gustavo's concern for "the pastoral and ecclesial nature of the Good News." The creation of the Bartolomé de las Casas Center in Lima has helped to unify these concerns, and through it various study projects are carried on in close contact with the oppressed people of Latin America.

I once moderated a panel in which Gustavo and a well-known pacifist debated the issue of violence in Christian ethics. The pacifist had ready responses for every question; he had answered them so often that there was no pain, no anguish. Gustavo dealt with each question with pain and anguish. He wrestled with the moral dilemma that Christians might find that all other alternatives to violence had been exhausted. There were no pat answers. It was an ongoing struggle he shared with his listeners. It was authentic.

"Authentic" is a good word with which to describe Gustavo. His lectures ("always three points") employ no tricks, no verbal rhetoric, no professional snow jobs. Each point goes on the blackboard, the argument clearly developed with an opportunity for questions, before the subheadings are erased to make space for the next major point. References to history and to personal experience are cleanly interwoven. The polemic against bourgeois ideology and capitalist imperialism is direct when relevant, but not so strident as to cut off discussion. The openness to new ideas—Bonhoeffer, the "social gospel," the ordination of women—is genuine.

Example:

> Question: What do you think about women's ordination?
> Answer: I don't see any reason to refuse the ordination of
> women. This is also a new question for me, and an im-
> portant step in Christian consciousness. At the same
> time I have a preoccupation. I would not like that the
> ordination of women reinforce the "clericalism" in the
> church. Then our gains would be losses. [11]

Gustavo could spend all his time, if he chose to do so, lecturing at intellectual centers throughout the world to learned audi-
ences. He does not choose to do so. Most of the lecturing he does,
particularly at home, is to "the people," and notably to an annual
two week "summer course" in theology, given at the Catholic
University in Lima. Over 800 people come to this course every
summer, mostly lay folk. Since the government now realizes that
"theology" is a subversive topic, it is touch and go every spring
whether or not the upcoming summer course will be permitted,
the more so since Gustavo is long since *persona non grata* among
government officials.

The pressures on him are not only intellectual and political.
Many demands on his time are personal; he is a priest, and he
takes the priestly calling seriously. I know several people in New
York City who literally would not have survived without the pas-
toral help of this short, unprepossessing, eminently kind man.
There must be thousands of such people in Latin America.

He does not live in the pleasant university area in Lima, but
in a third-floor apartment over the Bartolomé de las Casas Center
in the Rimac slum area of Lima, where he spends the bulk of his
time. The quarters are spartan, though there is a roof where one
can sit in the evening—as if there were ever time to sit in the
evening. The second floor is the Center itself, with a sizeable
library (Gustavo's books for the most part), a study, a conference
room and kitchen, while the first floor of the building houses the
shop of a local merchant.

His recreational pleasures, as far as I have been able to discover, are two: he is fond of swimming, and one bonus to his frequent lecturing at Maryknoll Seminary in New York State is unlimited access to the pool; but even more than that, he is inordinately, intemperately, immoderately and ravenously fond of ice cream. Any flavor.

Our *Who's Who* simulation noted that Gustavo has an honorary degree from the Catholic University in Nijmegen. There may be others. But he wears such honors lightly. There is a well-verified story (though Gustavo is not the source) that Yale University voted to give him an honorary degree several years ago. But Yale requires that the recipient receive the degree in person and stipulates that the offer will be made only once. Gustavo just could not make it to New Haven that year. It was a matter of priorities. He had already agreed to lead a retreat for lay people the same weekend.

Where does Gustavo's story go from here? No biographer had better predict. We can assume that the political situation in Peru will make things increasingly difficult for him. But whatever course Peruvian history takes, one can predict at least the following: Gustavo will be found among the oppressed, whoever and wherever they are. If it comes to a choice between being there or writing another book, he will be there and the book will have to wait.

CHAPTER THREE

The First Act: Commitment to the Poor (praxis)

Many Christians . . . poor or rich . . . have deliberately and explicitly identified with the oppressed on our continent. . . . This is *the major fact* in the recent life of the Christian community in Latin America.[12]

Within a society where social classes conflict we are true to God when we side with the poor, the working classes, the despised races, the marginal cultures.[13]

It is through encounters with the poor and the exploited that we shall encounter the Lord.[14]

The criteria of any theology are its practical consequences, not its theoretical assumptions.[15]

Some theologies, as we have already noted, are formed in libraries, seminary classrooms, private studies. Gustavo's theology, after ample exposure to all that, was re-formed out of his involvement in combatting the oppression of the poor.

Christians cannot accept the oppression of the poor as tolerable. That many Christians have done so, and have even urged the oppressed to accept their situation (arguing that patience in this world will pay off in the next) is an ugly reality of which all Christians must repent. There is a sense of *urgency* in Gustavo's approach to these problems that is often lacking in the perspective of comfortably situated Christians.

One need not be a Christian to recognize widespread injustice and do battle with it: Gustavo's friend, Juan Luis Segundo, has particularly emphasized that it is a *pre*-theological conviction, available to anyone, that "the world should not be the way it is." But if one is a Christian, one can never condone the present unjust order, and one must be committed to its victims, the poor. *That is the starting point for everything else*—not abstract principles but commitment to the poor.

Sub-version or Super-version?

Gustavo's own discovery that poverty was the result of unjust social structures rather than lack of initiative by the poor, leads to a recognition that commitment to the poor will mean commitment to changing the social structures that exploit them. The recognition that evil is rooted in social structures and not just individual human hearts, means that "radical" changes are called for. The word "radical" comes from *radix*, which means "root;" to look at a problem "radically" is to try to get to the "root" of the problem. The root of the problem for Gustavo is that present social structures exploit the many poor for the sake of the few rich. The only effective way to deal with such structures is to "uproot" them, so that other structures can replace them. Deep-rooted problems call for deep-rooted remedies. One of Gustavo's statements (here re-cast as blank verse) makes the point:

> The Latin American poor
>   seek to eradicate their misery,
>   not ameliorate it;
> hence they choose
>   social revolution rather than reform,
>   liberation rather than development,
>   and
>   socialism rather than liberalization.[16]

Uprooting means turning things upside down, so that the powerful are divested of power and the poor are invested with power. Nothing "new" here, actually: Mary enunciated the theme two millenia ago:

> he has put down the mighty from their thrones,
> and exalted those of low degree;
> he has filled the hungry with good things,
> and the rich God has sent empty away.

(Luke 1:52–53)

To fulfill that mandate, Gustavo believes, calls for "sub-versive" action, and we must understand what he means. The base of the verb is *vertir*, to stand something on its head, in this case, to change the course of history. There are two possibilities: history can be changed "from below" (*sub-vertir*) by "sub-versive action," which means that the poor take charge of their own lives, or it can be changed "from above" (*super-vertir*) by "super-versive action," which means that the rich ensure that their position of privilege is not challenged. [17]

Gustavo has no doubt about which form of action the gospel demands.

The discussion can be concretized by looking at the difference between "development" and "liberation." Development schemes in the 1960's involved rich nations helping poor nations get on their feet by financial grants, loans, or outright gifts. The "Decade of Development," sponsored by the United Nations, sought to accelerate such activities, but at the end of the decade the gap between the rich and poor had *increased*: the rich had become richer and the poor had become poorer. Gustavo maintains that there is a causal relation: the rich get richer by exploiting the poor and keeping them that way. It is the rich nations that "develop," and they do so by dominating the poor nations. So there is this indictment:

1. Development is *tokenism*. It does not fundamentally change a system concerned about profits more than about persons, and is content with cosmetic "changes" that look impressive but do not really change anything.

2. Development is *exploitative*. "Aid" that goes to needy countries shores up the already repressive regimes in those countries, and is often linked with military aid to ensure "stability," which translated, means no unrest; which, translated yet again, means no chance for the poor. Accelerated industrialization in third world countries does not, according to Gustavo, lead to a better situation in those countries. On the contrary, the industrial nations use the poorer nations as a place to secure high profits through paying low wages and over-exploiting the ready labor supply.

3. Development is *paternalistic*. Those who pay the piper call the tune; decisions about what is "good for" Latin American countries are not made in Santiago or Lima or Buenos Aires, but in Washington or Bonn or London.

Development, in other words is super-versive. It changes superficially from above, rather than radically from below, and it does so in the interests of those on top, rather than those on the bottom.

> To reread history means *to remake history*. It means making history from below, and therefore, it will be a subversive history. History must be changed around, not from above but from below. There is no evil in being a subversive, struggling against the capitalist system, rather what is evil today is to be a "superversive," a support to the existing domination.[18]

So commitment to the poor is for the purpose of subversive action against a system that perpetuates injustice rather than overcoming it.

> Solidarity cannot limit itself to just saying no to the way things are arranged. It must be more than that. It must be an effort to forge a society in which the worker is not subordinated to the owner of the means of production, a society in which the assumption of social responsibility for political affairs will include social responsibility for real liberty and will lead to the emergence of a new social consciousness.
> Solidarity with the poor implies the transformation of the existing social order.[19]

The Three Kinds of "Poverty"

In Catholic circles, "poverty" is one of the evangelical counsels (along with chastity and obedience) and certain strains of Christian spirituality have exalted poverty in ways that condone its continuation. To overcome such semantic and existential temptation, Gustavo distinguishes three kinds of poverty.[20]

Material poverty is "the lack of economic goods necessary for a human life worthy of the name," a subhuman condition to be opposed always. *Spiritual poverty*, often seen as "an interior attitude of unattachment to the goods of this world," often leads, as

Gustavo puts it, "to comforting and tranquillizing conclusions." One can possess many material goods, according to this reading, so long as one is not "attached" to them, and one need not be concerned about those who lack material goods, since material goods should not dominate one's life.

But there is a *biblical understanding* of poverty as well. "In the Bible, poverty is a *scandalous condition* inimical to human dignity and therefore contrary to the will of God." The prophets and Jesus inveigh against the oppressiveness that results when the rich exploit the poor. But the Bible also understands poverty as *spiritual childhood*, an attitude opposed to pride or self-sufficiency, synonymous with faith and trust in the Lord.

So when the gospel says that the poor are blessed, it is not condoning poverty on the grounds that its injustice will someday be overcome in the kingdom of God. Rather:

> the elimination of the exploitation and poverty that prevent the poor from being fully human has begun; a Kingdom of justice which goes even beyond what they could have hoped for has begun. They are blessed because the coming of the Kingdom will put an end to their poverty by creating a world of brotherhood.[21]

Gustavo feels that the biblical notions of material poverty as a "scandalous condition," and spiritual poverty as "an attitude of openness to God and spiritual childhood," come together in an understanding of *poverty as a commitment of solidarity and protest*.

The Christian is not to idealize poverty but to protest against it: "Christian poverty, as an expression of love, is solidarity *with the poor* and is a protest *against poverty*." This kind of identification with the poor means that "to be with the oppressed is to be against the oppressor," and that in turn means political engagement in a struggle against the structures of society that are designed to keep the poor poor so that the rich can become richer.

Praxis: A Shorthand Term for a Long Range Concern

We are already talking about praxis, another key word that is subject to semantic abuse. It is not quite the equivalent of "prac-

tice." It points to *the ongoing interplay of reflection and action*. When
we act, reflect on the action, and then act in a new way on the
basis of our reflection (or when we reflect, and then act, and then
reflect in a new way on the basis of our action) we are illustrating
praxis. It is the heart of the Christian endeavor, which is always
tempted to remain theoretical, or to get "involved" unthinkingly
and become irrelevant, quixotic, or downright evil.

So stated, there is nothing particularly new about emphasiz-
ing praxis. Christians always struggle with the tension between
reflection and action, work and study, prayer and picketing. Even
the classic statement by Anselm, a medieval theologian, "I believe in order that I may understand," is a praxis utterance, affirming that reflection (understanding) can only take place in the
midst of commitment (believing).

What *is* new is that Gustavo's praxis is not just any old praxis,
but rather *the praxis of the poor*. The distinction is between a methodology and the methodology's frame of reference. As far as methodology goes,

> Liberation theology has maintained that active commitment
> to liberation comes first and theology develops from it. . . .
> Liberation theology reflects on and from within the complex
> and fruitful relationship between theory and practice.[22]

There is much agreement that commitment precedes theological
reflection, and that it is developed in the "complex and fruitful
relationship between theory and practice." Anselm committed
himself to love God, a God found in the midst of ontological
reflection.

But it is methodology's frame of reference that provides the
parting of the ways:

> Liberation theology's second central intuition is that God is a
> liberating God, revealed only in the concrete historical context
> of liberation of the poor and oppressed. This second point is
> inseparable from the first. . . . It is not enough to know that
> praxis must precede reflection; we must also realize that the
> historical subject of that praxis is the poor—the people who
> have been excluded from the pages of history. Without the

poor as subject, theology degenerates into academic exper-
tise.[23]

Gustavo, like Anselm, commits himself to love God, but Gustavo's God is found not in the midst of ontological reflection, but
in the midst of the poor.

Unless we understand praxis as the praxis of the poor, we will
co-opt Gustavo's theology into a non-threatening middle-class
version.

Two Latin American Understandings that Lead to North American Misunderstandings

As we begin to explore what it means to make this commitment to the poor, two aspects emerge that are almost universally
misunderstood in North American discussion of liberation theology. These are the use of Marx and the use of violence.

The use of Marx—Because of the almost pathological fear of
Karl Marx in North America, we must take note of the development of Gustavo's interest in Marx and the relationship of Marx
to his theology.

Gustavo first encountered Marx's writings during his student
days at San Marcos University, both as a result of sheer intellectual
curiosity and in relation to his political activity as a student.
These initial encounters were largely theoretical, and consisted of
reading a few of Marx's writings as well as the basic work of the
Peruvian Marxist Mariátegui. During this time Gustavo was also
active in Christian groups on the campus and saw no incompati-
bility between his "religious" and "political" involvements. The
interest in Marx continued at Louvain through courses with Franz
Gregoire, who saw Marx mainly in a Hegelian light but exposed
Gustavo particularly to the writings of the early Marx. While
doing theology at Lyon, Gustavo studied with French Jesuits who
were taking Marx more seriously than most of their theological
contemporaries, and they pointed him to a deeper immersion in
Marx's writings and contemporary Marxist thinkers such as
Gramsci.

From the time of his first teaching at Lima in 1961, Gustavo lectured on the issues raised by a confrontation between Christian and Marxist thought, always, as he comments, with a "pastoral" concern for students who were being forced to confront both points of view in their daily lives.

How has this exposure to Marx affected Gustavo's theology? Perhaps Marx's most important contribution has been to provide tools for social analysis that *help to make sense of the Latin American situation*. This does not mean accepting Marx's whole world view; Gustavo's world view is provided by biblical and Catholic Christianity. But it does mean letting certain concepts of Marx inform how we approach injustice and exploitation in the world in which the God of the Bible has placed us.

First example: Marx employs the concept of *class struggle* to understand how our economic system works. In that system there are workers and owners, proletariat and bourgeoisie, oppressed and oppressors. The categories differ; what remains constant is that those on top want to keep what they have and get more, while those on the bottom want more than they have and get less. Both reactions are perfectly natural, given the components of the system. Those on the bottom are not treated as persons by those on the top, but as commodities, capable of producing a certain amount of labor. What that labor is worth is finally determined by the owners. If there are only a few jobs available, and many workers are competing for those jobs, the wages will be competitively low, perhaps even below a living wage. But the workers will still compete strenuously for the jobs, since if one is starving any wage is better than no wage.

When Gustavo looks at how Latin American society operates, the above is an almost letter-perfect description of what he sees. There *is* a "struggle" between the "classes," between rich and poor, between oppressors and oppressed.[24] Marx did not invent class struggle, he merely observed it and described it.

By any Christian standard, the terms of the struggle are wrong. The benefits derived from this struggle should not be so overwhelmingly advantageous to the rich and so overwhelmingly destructive to the poor. So Christians must enter the class struggle on the side of the poor.

One cannot help noticing an important convergence between such an analysis and the "good news" of the gospel. Listen to Jesus:

> The Spirit of the Lord is upon me,
> because he has anointed me to preach *good news to the poor*,
> He has sent me to proclaim *release to the captives*
> and recovering of sight to the blind,
> to *set at liberty those who are oppressed* . . .
>
> (Luke 4:18, italics added)

At this point, the message of Marx and the message of the gospel are strikingly similar.

Second example: Marx points out that the evil that needs to be combatted is not just the evil of a few individuals but *the evil of the system as a whole*. Capitalism is evil not because there are nasty individuals on boards of directors scheming to find ways to make children starve. However, Marx says, decisions made in good faith by boards of directors will tend, *by the very nature of the system*, to produce greater wealth for the few and greater poverty for the many, and thus compound injustice. For the system to "work," profits have to assume priority over persons. It is not enough to get a few highly placed individuals to have a "change of heart" (or even "find Jesus") since they are also trapped by the system and accountable to it. Conclusion: the system itself must be changed.

This also should have a familiar ring to readers of the gospel, with its vision of a new order, a new society, "a new heaven and a new earth," in which the poor do not remain poor, in which the mighty are put down from their thrones and those of low degree exalted—an image that originates not with Marx but with Mary. Paul's talk about the principalities and powers of darkness attests to the same thing. So once again, Marx's analysis drives us back to the Bible, and to a commitment to the poor with whom the biblical God so clearly sides, working to see that they, rather than boards of directors, make the final decisions about their own lives.

There are at least three things about a Christian reaction to Karl Marx that will help us to hear Gustavo fairly:

1. The importance of an idea lies not in who said it, but in whether or not it accurately describes the world in which we live. If it does not, we need not take it seriously even if it has been propounded by a theologian; if it does, we must take it seriously even if it has been propounded by a Karl Marx.

> What happens is that we can't be with the poor of Latin America without calling upon social analysis using terms like injustice, exploitation, exploiting class and class struggle to explain what is happening. To use certain notions to explain a reality does not mean agreeing with the determined [*sic*: determinist?] philosophical positions postulated by Marxism.[25]

2. When an insight is found in the Bible and also in Marx, its presence in Marx does not invalidate its presence in the Bible. The fact that Marx preached liberty for the oppressed does not render suspect Jesus' declaration of the same truth, nor does it render suspect a similar declaration on the lips of Jesus' followers. Jesus preached liberty for the oppressed 1800 years before Marx was even born; and he got it straight from the book of Isaiah, written at least 700 years before that. To dismiss contemporary calls for the liberty of the oppressed as "communist-inspired" is not only perverse thinking but faulty chronology.

3. There is a radical side to the Christian tradition that has been submerged for centuries and also long antedated Marx. Theologians in the early centuries affirmed, as Gustavo reminds us, "that if persons are in extreme need, they have the right to take from the riches of others what they themselves need. This is a very revolutionary attitude." And as he also reminds us, "This is a classical, not a Marxist idea."[26]

So Gustavo reads Marx, applies Marx, criticizes Marx, and teaches Marx, especially in terms of what Latin Americans might learn from him for carrying on a "gospel-inspired" Christian struggle.

A test. See if the following analysis now makes sense:

> External dependence and internal domination characterize the
> social structure of Latin America. This is why only a class
> analysis will permit us to see what is really at play in the
> opposition of oppressed countries and dominating coun-
> tries. . . . All this will lead us to understand the social for-
> mation of Latin America as a dependent capitalism and to
> foresee the necessary strategy to get out of that situation.
>   Only the transcending of a society divided into classes, a
> political power at the service of the great popular majorities,
> and the elimination of private appropriation of wealth pro-
> duced by human work can give us the foundations of a society
> that would be more just. It is for this reason that the elabora-
> tion in a historical project of a new society in Latin America
> takes more and more frequently the path of socialism.[27]

The problem of violence—The most frequent misunderstanding
of liberation theologians is that they "glorify violence." It is important to dispel the misunderstanding.[28]

1. All Latin Americans, Gustavo not excepted, are in a situation that is *already violent*. It is part of their daily (and nightly)
life. They do not initiate a consideration of violence; it is already
there.

2. Gustavo has succinctly defined the kinds of violence that
must be distinguished from one another.

> In Latin America, we have three types of violence. The first is
> the *institutionalized violence* of the present social order; the sec-
> ond, the *repressive violence* which defends the first, keeping in
> power the ruling regimes; and the third, *counter-violence*. To
> me, counter-violence is the least of the evils.[29]

Many North Americans and Europeans are not even aware of the
first and most pervasive violence, the *institutionalized violence* that
condemns tens of thousands of people to suffering, starvation and
death. Violence is at work there, even if a gun is never fired and
an army never marches. As Gustavo puts it, "The greatest violence in Latin America is not that of a man heading for the
mountains with a rifle, but institutionalized injustice."[30] We have
a little recognition of the *repressive violence* visible in the brutal
Latin American dictatorships, though we are not usually aware

that many of them survive only because of the support of the U.S. and Western Europe. If we saw the extent of these first two kinds of violence more clearly, we might better understand why despairing people are sometimes tempted to employ counter-violence against them.

3. Appeals to *counter-violence* come only "when all else fails," and when, having "counted the cost," it appears that to refrain from counter-violence would perpetuate more injustice by the *status quo* than an attempt to overthrow it. Nicaragua had forty years of the first two kinds of violence, and a few months of counter-violence as the Sandinistas finally overthrew the tyrannical regime. Many Christians elsewhere criticized the Sandinistas for "resorting to violence," but never protested the Somoza regime's much more extreme violence over four decades.

4. Gustavo's concern is to bring about change by peaceful means. He works with what he calls "the non-violent people." He does not call indiscriminately for violent revolution. He does call for revolution. The decision about whether revolution will be violent or non-violent will not be made by Gustavo and his friends. It will be made by those with power. If they voluntarily share that power with the poor there will be peaceful change. If they resist sharing power and continue to destroy the poor, then they will create a condition in which appeal to "the last resort" may be all that is left in the name of justice.

5. Those who consistently repudiate violence and criticize *all* theologians (about 98.6% of the present crop) who are willing to consider violence "as a last resort," are entitled to press the case. Those who press the case only against liberation theologians are operating with hidden, if not devious, agendas, and need not be taken seriously.

The Poor and the Church

The first act, commitment to the poor, is not ethereal, but very earthy and practical. How does the church fit in to this?

As we have seen, the church in Latin America historically sided with the rich, and consoled the poor with promises of heaven. Such twisting of the gospel is now widely challenged. Since Medellín, there has been much talk, and even some action, about the church as "the church of the poor," the church in which the poor are not relegated to second or third class citizenship, but are central to its life. Gustavo has tried to push the discussion still further. "It is not enough," he says frequently in conversation, "to be the church of the poor; we must become the poor church." If this means turning down some handsome donations from the United States, that may not be too heavy a price to pay for integrity, and unless the church embraces poverty in the way Jesus himself did, it can hardly claim to be the contemporary manifestation of his body. Only by real *solidarity with the poor*, can the church engage in significant *protest against poverty*. There may be a still better way of putting it. The task is not so much "making the church poor" as seeing to it that *the poor of the world become the church*, an approach Gustavo has recently been proposing. Wherever the poor are, there Christ is; wherever Christ is, there the church should be. So doors must open, walls must crumble. A new church might emerge out of the rubble.

A further step was taken at Puebla, encapsulated in a phrase from Document 18 (the document on which Gustavo worked), that the church must make "a preferential option for the poor," taking sides explicitly and not only implicitly. This could become the most significant single commitment of the Puebla meetings. It will be hard to translate the phrase into a living reality, but it presents the greatest challenge the church will face in our time.

"A preferential option for the poor" is not made for the purpose of excluding others. As the poor are liberated from their scandalous poverty, new conditions will be created in which the non-poor will no longer be able to act as oppressors, and new relationships will be possible in a community in which all can share. So to start with a preferential option for the poor is finally to reach out to include the non-poor as well. To start at the opposite end, with a preferential option for the non-poor, as the church has done for centuries, cuts the church off from the poor, since the concern of the non-poor will always be to keep the poor from threatening them, and creative relationship will remain impossible.

Finally, the poor must become the articulators and the practitioners of the gospel. The rest of us may not do it "for them." That would only be a new kind of paternalism.

> The preaching of the gospel will be truly liberating when the poor themselves are the preachers. Then of course the proclamation of the gospel will be a stumbling block, it will be a gospel 'unacceptable to society' and expressed in the vernacular. Thus the Lord will speak to us. Only by listening to this voice will we recognize him as our savior.[31]

> We will not have an authentic theology of liberation until the oppressed are able to express themselves freely and creatively in society and as the People of God.[32]

That will not make church life simple. But it will certainly keep it from being dull.

CHAPTER FOUR

The Second Act: Theology as "Critical Reflection on Praxis in the Light of the Word of God" (method)

> In this context [identification with the struggles of the oppressed] theology will be a critical reflection in and on historical praxis in confrontation with the Word of the Lord lived and accepted in faith.[33]
>
> Faith in God does not consist in asserting [God's] existence but rather in acting for [on God's behalf].[34]
>
> The God of the lords and masters is not the same God in whom the poor and exploited believe.[35]
>
> Any claim to non-involvement in politics . . . is nothing but a subterfuge to keep things as they are.[36]

Theology is "the second act." Few themes resound more frequently in Gustavo's writings than this assertion. The "first act," as we have seen, is commitment to the poor, and this involves praxis, the ongoing interplay between action and reflection, reflection and action. Theology is *"critical reflection on praxis* in the light of the Word of God." In this chapter we will examine the italicized portion of that definition; in the next chapter we will italicize the other portion and repeat the process. By itself, the phrase "critical reflection on praxis" may sound redundant, as though theology were "critical reflection on 'reflection and action.'" But that is descriptively the case; theology is a kind of *second* reflection, so to speak, examining what has already been going on, but now examining it from a theological perspective

(in Gustavo's phrase "in the light of the Word of God," that portion of the definition we are temporarily bracketing.)

The best way to understand Gustavo's methodology is to compare his way of doing theology with our own, which he calls the "dominant theology." And the fairest way is to let Gustavo himself be our guide, since (as we have already seen) he was first educated to do "our" kind of theology, so that he knows both kinds from within.[37]

"Dominant theology" is the product of affluent, largely European, cultures. It attempts to respond to the questions of the *non-believer*, the person whose faith has been shattered by the Enlightenment, or the rise of modern science, or other historical movements that have rendered traditional faith either impossible or unimportant. Bonhoeffer's problem, how to speak of God in "a world come of age,"—a world that has gained maturity and autonomy—is a good example of this theology at work.

Gustavo's writings give increasing attention to Bonhoeffer, whom he treats with great respect. But our issue can be joined more clearly by considering another European theologian, Johann Baptist Metz.[38] Metz is dealing with the problems raised by the Enlightenment, which, by stressing that the modern world has gained autonomy, forced Christianity to retreat from the public and social realm, retaining only the "privatized" realm of interior faith. The "theology of secularization" played that game and settled for two realms, one public and the other private (elsewhere called "the distinction of planes" by Gustavo) while new versions of "liberal theology" settled for an uncritical conformism to the world. In opposition to both of these Metz has called for a "political theology" that de-privatizes the faith, returning it to the public realm, but in a critical fashion. Jesus' death, for example, was due to his conflict with the political powers of his time; theology, as the "dangerous memory" of such biblical realities, must be recovered by theologians today whom Metz feels have been too remote and should "allow themselves to be interrupted by the mute suffering of a people."

Gustavo, after affirming that this is admirable, and that

"Metz has exploited a very rich vein for theology," raises two questions:

1. He feels that because Metz is "far from the revolutionary ferment of the Third World countries, he cannot penetrate the situation of dependency, injustice, and exploitation in which most of the human family finds itself."[39] Since Metz has not directly experienced these confrontations and conflicts—or the consequent aspiration to liberation that emerges from them—his analysis remains "rather abstract"; it would be helped by more attention to the social sciences, and especially certain aspects of Marxism.

2. Despite Metz' important rejection of the political conformism of the "theology of secularization," Gustavo feels that he has not completely shaken it off, and that he extrapolates too easily from the European situation, assuming "the universal existence of a secularized world and the privatization of the faith."[40] That is simply not a description of Latin America, where, by contrast, religion has both a central and a public role, albeit tragically pro-establishment. So one should not transplant Metz' analysis elsewhere and assume that it is descriptive or prescriptive. It is not helpful in the Latin American context. (This is an important reminder against those critics who charge that liberation theology is nothing but "transplanted European political theology.") Those who follow Metz must not be naive about the baleful influence of advanced capitalist society, nor must they work within too narrow an ecclesiastical framework.

Metz hears such concerns, and his most recent book, *Faith in History and Society* (Seabury Press), provides the next round in the exchange. Gustavo treats Metz' theology with respect ("a fertile effort to think the faith through") but it should be clear from the above remarks why he does not find Metz relevant to his own situation, and why he has sought to provide another "theological perspective" in contrast to "dominant theology."

This other "theological perspective" is, of course, liberation theology. By contrast to "dominant theology" it is the product of the poor in third world countries, and of exploited groups in rich countries. It is not attempting to respond to the questions of the non-believer, but of the *non-person*. By this term, Gustavo describes the poor, exploited individuals whose personhood is not acknowledged by the surrounding social order, those who are often "non-cultured," usually from the lower classes, possibly illiterate, always "marginated" from the rest of society. Such people are often "religious" (in a way the "non-believers" are not) but their questions are addressed not to the religious world so much as to the political-social-economic world. They question the whole society that perpetuates such misery for people like themselves, and they believe that revolutionary transformation is the only way left to humanize a dehumanized social order that creates non-persons. In their situation, the theological problem is not how to proclaim God in a "world come of age," but how to proclaim to non-persons that God is personal, and that all human beings are truly sisters and brothers.

To make such a proclamation, it is not enough to have developed an up-to-date metaphysics. The proclaimers, i.e. the theologians, affirm the personhood of non-persons not by a theory, but by *entering into solidarity with them*, and working to overthrow situations that perpetuate their non-personhood. Las Casas did this four centuries ago; Christians must do it again today.

To "do" theology in this way means to appropriate some new tools, particularly the social sciences, in order to understand what forces are at work perpetuating injustice, and how those forces can be challenged. We have already seen why Marx is important in this undertaking. But just as important, methodologically, is a new way of relating reflection and action. Gustavo describes it as a recognition that *knowledge is linked to transformation*. True knowledge of reality leads us to change that reality. Theological knowledge must share in that transforming impetus. Theological reflection must embolden people to deeper commitment and further action; in the Latin American situation, this will mean being "on the side of the oppressed classes and dominated peoples." It will be "critical reflection on praxis" that not only springs from engagement but leads to newer and deeper engagement. It will be "a theology which does not stop with reflecting on the world, but tries to be part of the process through which the world is transformed."

This is clearly a break with a "dominant theology" that tries to interpret the world but not necessarily to change it, at least not radically. The break is *not only theological but also political*. Not only are the interrogators different—the non-believers and the non-persons—but the situation of those who respond is also different.

Dominant theology responds "from above," from the position of the privileged, the cultured, the affluent, the bourgeois; liberation theology responds "from below," from the "underside of history," from the position of the oppressed, the marginated, the exploited. Dominant theology has largely been written by "those with white hands" (Leonardo Boff's image); liberation theology, only beginning to be written, must be written by those with dark-skinned, often crushed, hands. Dominant theology has links "with western culture, the white race, the male sex and the bourgeois class"; liberation theology is "linked with 'the condemned of the earth,' the poor, the marginalized races, despised cultures and sex, exploited classes." Dominant theology has tended to affirm many achievements of our culture—individualism, rationalism, the bourgeois spirit; liberation theology, acknowledging that such "gains" have been gains for some, also sees that they have been used as vehicles for imposing dependency on others:

> The system that meant intellectual and political freedom and economic opportunity for Europe and the United States . . . brought only new forms of oppression and exploitation to the common people of Latin America.[41]

The circle always comes around to action. A new perspective, if it is only a "perspective" becomes a betrayal. It is not enough to re-read history, or even to re-read the Bible, from "the underside of history." All that will remain an academic exercise *unless the re-reading leads to a re-making*. And the dynamics of that are clear:

> Re-making history means subverting it, that is to say "turning
> it upside down" and seeing it from below instead of from
> above.[42]

Liberation theology, then, reads history from the perspective
of the "losers" rather than the "winners," because it is standing
where the losers are, and insisting that the losers need not remain
losers. To us this sounds like a lonely place to be, until we remem-
ber that the majority of the human family is there, and that oc-
casionally in the past other Christians have stood there too—certain members of the early church, medieval and reformation
"sectarians," Bartolomé de Las Casas, and a few others. So this re-
reading is a recovery of a certain part of Christian history, as well
as a repudiation of much of the rest of Christian history. It taps
into a stream, as Gustavo puts it in a vivid image, "welling up
periodically in the desert of academic theology."[43]

A useful way to contrast the two perspectives is to observe
how each evaluates an event common to both. Let us use Vatican
II's document on "The Church and the World Today" as a case
study.

Both theologies share a perception that Vatican II helped the
Catholic church to come out of its self-imposed Catholic ghetto
and confront the contemporary world. They share a perception
that the document on "The Church and the World Today" is the
best instance of this confrontation with modernity, and that certain questions confronting the secular world were taken seriously:
questions of atheism, human rights, reason, progress, and so on.

But here the shared perceptions cease. The questions that
Gustavo and people like him have to deal with every day were
ignored by the Council; to that extent the Council was *not* speaking to "the modern world" but only to a small portion of it, the
well-to-do bourgeois upper middle class portion. For while Vatican II broke new ground, it was mainly the ground inhabited by
Europeans and North Americans. Seen from the perspective of
Latin Americans, however, the Council did not really hear the
cries of "the wretched of the earth." The true interlocutors, in

other words, to whom the Council was responding, were the non-believers rather than the non-persons. Vatican II, Gustavo concedes, engaged in an "acknowledgement of the modern world's values," but was guilty of "disregard of its [modern world's] defects. . . . Poverty, injustice, inequality, and class conflict were barely touched upon."[44] Even more sternly:

> There is no serious criticism of the effects of domination by monopolistic capitalism on the working classes, particularly in the poor countries. Nor is there any clear realization of the new forms of oppression and exploitation perpetrated in the name of these modern world values.[45]

So the claim that the Council opened up to the modern world must be qualified by noting that so far the opening extends only in the direction of the bourgeois world.

Most of us who inhabit the world have assumed that since the church was speaking to us, it was speaking to all. Gustavo demonstrates how limited our perspective really is. That is clear gain. Painful, but clear.

CHAPTER FIVE

A Closer Look at the Second Act (content)

The primacy of God and the grace of faith give theological work its *raison d'être*.[46]

To opt for the poor, to be identified with their lot, to share their destiny, means a desire to make of history genuine community for all people. It means accepting the free gift of becoming children of God and opting for the cross of Christ in the hope and joy of his Resurrection.[47]

What is really at work is not just a greater rationality of economic activity or a better social organization, but, rather justice and love working through these. . . . liberating praxis, in the measure that it starts from an authentic solidarity with the poor and the oppressed, will be, in short, *a praxis of love* . . . of neighbor and therein, of love of Christ who identified himself with the least of humanity.[48]

The political commitment to liberation [is placed] in the perspective of the free gift of the total liberation brought by Christ.[49]

Gustavo's theology arises out of commitment to the poor. Its implications for both reflection and action are *radical* (getting at the *radix* or "root" of the matter) and *revolutionary* (demanding widespread change as the condition for a humane future).

Those who dislike radical and revolutionary ideas, particularly when connected with theology, often suggest that Gustavo does not really have a "theology" at all, but merely a program for political action (worse than that, *socialist* political action . . .) over which a thin veneer of "God-talk" is spread. Others concede that it may be a "theology" of sorts, but surely not a "Christian theology," since it is so obsessively preoccupied with the "here and now" that it excludes recognition of the "beyond," or of mystery, or the spiritual dimension of human existence, let alone such themes as God, Christ, salvation, sin, the church, the Kingdom of God or eschatology.

The approach is convenient for those who dislike Gustavo's politics; if they can show that he is unorthodox or heretical, they can thereby discredit the politics.

In this chapter we shall try to show that such a critique is ill-informed, if not perverse, and that those who attempt it are likely to be hoist on their own petard, since the facts do not warrant it. The way to rebut the criticism (in addition to asking the critics to do Gustavo the favor of actually reading his writings) is to concentrate on the second half of Gustavo's definition of theology, "critical reflection on praxis *in the light of the Word of God.*" In so doing we are, in effect, moving from *method* to *content*. When we ask *what* he affirms (as we shall now do) as well as *how* he affirms it (as we have just done) we discover that his position is not only "theology" but "Christian theology" as well.

If the method is radical, the content is also radical, but in a slightly different way. Gustavo does strongly re-appropriate the "great themes" of classical Christianity (that the critics accuse him of "reducing" to ethics or "horizontalism") but he does so by getting to their "root," whittling away the safe, tame, comfortable bourgeois efflorescence we have cultivated around them, so that the great Christian affirmations themselves are liberated from our bourgeois grasp, and we are forced to look once again at them in their original and naked and alarming power. We must not be deceived about this; the words are often the same, but the realities to which the words point—God, Christ, sin, salvation—are now being viewed "from below" rather than "from above," and so they become very different from how we have known them, but much more like the way they were originally known.

In the light of these considerations, we will sample a few of

the things Gustavo affirms about the content of the Christian
faith.

The Three Levels of Liberation

Let us first clear the air about the key term "liberation" itself.
Gustavo is insistent that there are three levels of liberation, and
only when they are all present is the full meaning of the term
before us.[50]

The *first* level is the aspiration of oppressed peoples for liberation from all the political, social, economic (and often ecclesiastical) structures that oppress and destroy them. We have already
given attention to this.

The *second* level is liberation from a view of history that teaches
that persons can do nothing about their own destiny, and must
accept whatever fate (or providence) assigns them. The paren-
thesis is important, for much of the Christian message to oppressed peoples has been: be patient if things are not going well
for you; God has put you where you are for reasons best known to
him; you will be rewarded after death if you do not make trouble,
listen to communists, or join a labor union; if your blessed Savior
could endure suffering on the cross, who are you to complain,
whose woes are so trifling compared to his? Gustavo emphasizes
that the gospel urges people to take initiatives in defying those
who profit from injustice, and in working to improve their situation and that of their neighbors.

The *third* level of liberation emphasizes that

> Christ is presented as the one who brings us liberation. Christ
> the Savior liberates us from sin, which is the ultimate root of
> all disruption of friendship and of all injustice and oppression.
> Christ makes us truly free, that is to say, he enables us to live
> in communion with him; and this is the basis for all human
> community.[51]

If Gustavo devotes less quantitative attention to this third level
than to the other two, it is for the perfectly good reason that most
other theologies devote inordinate attention to it; its importance

is widely acknowledged. But Gustavo still gives much more attention to it than his critics seem to realize. He talks at great length about "the spirituality of liberation," as we shall see, while maintaining that "spirituality" cannot be talked about by itself; the three levels all imply one another. The danger comes when concern for spirituality is isolated so that it leads to neglect of concern for political and economic and physical well-being as conditions of full liberation. Only people with full stomachs can think that way.

> Liberation is another word for salvation. Liberation is living out one's salvation in the concrete historical conditions of today. Theology of liberation is not a theology of political liberation, although political liberation is one aspect of salvation.[52]

Jesus Christ the Liberator

The touchstone of any Christian theology is the place it accords to Jesus of Nazareth. We will summarize one of Gustavo's many affirmations of the centrality of Jesus Christ as "the full manifestation of the God who is love."[53]

1. *Jesus is the Christ.* Christians believe in a person, not a message. That person, the Jew Jesus, "killed for being a subversive," is the Christ, the Messiah, the Son. The God in whom we believe is the God of whom Jesus is the Son. Jesus came on earth from God, and he "is also the one who will come; he is the future of our history."

2. *Christ the Liberator.* Jesus Christ is "God become poor," born in a social milieu of poverty, choosing to live with the poor, who proclaimed the kingdom of God revealed in his coming. "It is a kingdom of justice and liberation which should be established and built from the perspective of the poor, the oppressed, and the marginated peoples of history." Proclamation of this kingdom cost Jesus his life.

3. *The New Covenant.* "Jesus himself is the new covenant." In him God becomes the God of all peoples. He is "the principle of interpretation of the Scriptures. In Jesus Christ we find God; in

the human word we find the Word of God, in historical events we
recognize the fulfillment of the promise."

In him "a new creation is brought about." The death of Jesus
is a consequence of his struggle for justice, but it "broke open"
the limits of his contemporaries understanding of him, so that
the resurrection could give "a qualitatively new insight into the
universality of the sonship and daughtership and brotherhood and
sisterhood which Jesus had announced." The subsequent Christian
message is always made in the light of this Easter faith.

4. *The Lord's Supper*. "The eucharist is a thanksgiving for these
historical events in which the love of God is revealed." But in
addition, "it is a confident and joyfully full opening to the future." Its celebration presupposes solidarity with the poor, for
without this it is impossible to understand the death and resurrection of the servant of Yahweh.

The implications of all this are clear:

> To believe in the God who is revealed in history and whose
> tent is pitched in history, *means to live in that tent*, that is to
> say, in Jesus Christ, and from that perspective, to proclaim
> the liberating love of God.[54]

So "Christology" is not so much a doctrine as a proclamation
of God's love in ways that demand our enlistment in the cause of
liberation.

The Kingdom of God and Human Effort

Gustavo insists that we cannot talk about the kingdom of God
as outside of history, in a "sacred history" isolated from human,
profane history. *History is one*: creation and salvation belong together, and God's engagement with people is in their own situation. The "new creation," a gift of God, is a new creation "in
Christ"; it is within the realm where Christ dwells, the realm of
human history, so we can participate in that new creation within
our history.

There is a clear biblical imperative to fight against injustice,
and the Bible claims that God engages in the struggle to over-

come oppression. The kingdom is a gift, but our response must be aligned with carrying out the purposes for which that gift stands. Gustavo affirms, along with Isaiah, that "Righteousness shall yield peace and its fruit [shall] be quietness and confidence forever."[55] What does it mean to affirm that?

> It presupposes the defense of the rights of the poor, punishment of the oppressors, a life free from the fear of being enslaved by others, the liberation of the oppressed. Peace, justice, love, and freedom are not private realities; they are not only internal attitudes. They are social realities, implying a historical liberation.[56]

To be part of the effort that God initiates and will crown, means that we can provide signs of the coming kingdom: "The struggle for a just world in which there is no oppression, servitude, or alienated work will signify the coming of the Kingdom."[57]

An eschatological perspective enables us to avoid equating human achievements with the kingdom of God. "Eschatological promises are being fulfilled throughout history, but this does not mean that they can be identified clearly and completely with one or another social reality; their liberating effect goes far beyond the forseeable and opens up new and unsuspected possibilities."[58]

A new political-social-economic order is not the same as the kingdom of God, which is finally God's gift. *But there are connections between them.* We can create human utopias (and "utopia" is not a pejorative term to Gustavo) which are not the kingdom but can play a role in helping us respond to the kingdom:

> The Gospel does not provide a utopia for us; this is a human work. The Word is a free gift of the Lord. But the Gospel is not alien to the historical plan; on the contrary, the human plan and the gift of God imply each other. The Word is the foundation and meaning of all human experience; this foundation is attested to and this meaning is concretized through human actions.[59]

Since "the Kingdom and social injustice are incompatible," we can affirm with Gustavo that the struggle for justice is also the struggle for the kingdom of God.

God's Love and "Class Struggle"

Let us press the argument by relating it to our earlier discussion. How, from a Christian perspective can one talk, as Gustavo talks, about Christians taking sides in the "class struggle," and even more about *God* taking sides? Surely God is the God of all people, not a God who "takes sides" with one class against another. Gustavo is aware of the dilemma: "How can we reconcile the *universality* of charity with the option for a *particular* social class?"[60]

He responds that there are two realities we cannot avoid: (1) class struggle is a fact, and (2) neutrality is impossible. What enlists people like Gustavo in the class struggle is not a concern to perpetuate class struggle but to *overcome* it. To ignore class struggle, or seek to remain "above" it, ensures its continuation; those who seek "neutrality" will *de facto* support the oppressors in power. Inaction is action on behalf of the *status quo*.

> To participate in class struggle not only is not opposed to universal love; this commitment is today the necessary and inescapable means of making this love concrete. For this participation is what leads to a classless society without owners and dispossessed, without oppressors and oppressed. In dialectical thinking, reconciliation is the overcoming of conflict. The communion of paschal joy passes through confrontation and the cross.[61]

So much for us. But what about God? Surely God does not take sides in this way. But Gustavo's belief is the opposite. God does take sides. The belief is not Gustavo's invention; it is the biblical belief, as we shall presently see. It is an expression of God's *universal* love that within our historical situation God will provisionally take sides with some and against others, so that present inequities may be overcome and the full possibilities of personhood opened for all. To say that God loves *all* people, means that those who thwart love must be opposed, so that their ability to perpetuate structures of oppression, which keep people separated from love of one another and of God, can be overcome.

The biblical God acts through specific human beings and historical events to extend the sway of the divine will.

So history is an arena of *conflict*. And in an arena of conflict, sides must be taken. Siding with the poor and the oppressed is the historical means through which obstacles created by the rich and the oppressors can be overcome, and God's love can embrace all.

The God of the Bible

The history of biblical interpretation is notorious for the degree to which its readers highlight those portions that buttress their own social philosophy and filter out those portions that challenge it. All of us do this, frequently unaware of what we are doing. So it is important to have our latent presuppositions exposed.

One could almost assume that the Bible read by liberation theologians and the Bible read by middle-class Christians were two different books, containing similar texts but yielding utterly different messages. When North Americans encounter third world biblical interpretation, they are likely to react, "Those people are biased; their own situation conditions their reading of Scripture . . ." Such a charge is appropriate only if it continues, " . . . and so does ours." Nobody approaches Scripture *de novo*; we bring things *to* the reading, as well as drawing things *from* the reading. But it is not enough to say: they read it one way, we read it another, end of discussion. *For one way of reading may be closer to the actual meaning than another*. Liberation theologians sometime talk (in a jawbreaking phrase) about "the epistemological privilege of the struggling poor" in reading Scripture. They mean that there is a privileged or advantageous way of understanding the Bible that is granted to the struggling poor and denied to the rich, because the struggling poor are closer to the situation of the biblical writers than the rich. Most of the biblical writers were themselves oppressed, writing to the oppressed in situations of oppression. Those in similar situations today are likely to have a better understanding of what the biblical writers are saying than those of us in very different situations, since they are attuned to the biblical message in ways we are not. If the message is "good news to the poor," the poor are likely to hear it affirmatively, while the rich look for ways to avoid its message.

There are a number of passages that are central to Gustavo's response to the Bible, but his theology is not based on a few proof-text passages, a game everybody can play. The Exodus story, for example, is central, but for him the truth that God acts *for* "slaves" and *against* oppressive rulers is not limited to the book of Exodus, but is central to the prophets, the gospels and the epistles. It *is* "the biblical story."

Among many passages used by Gustavo (and there are over 400 Scriptural references in *A Theology of Liberation* alone), let us look at one that states succinctly what he feels to be a pervasive theme throughout. In Jeremiah 22:13–16, the prophet is inveighing against the king (a familiar pastime of prophets). The king is living unjustly, building a palace with slave labor, paying no wages, and ignoring the plight of the poor and needy. Comparing the king to his father, Jeremiah asks:

> Did not your father eat and drink
> and do justice and righteousness?
> Then it was well with him.
> He judged the cause of the poor and needy;
> then it was well.
> *Is this not to know me?*
> says the Lord.

                                                        (vs. 15–16, italics added)

The question is rhetorical. To "know God," *is* to "do justice and righteousness," to judge "the cause of the poor and needy." Those who do that, know God; they are the believers. Those who do not do that, do not know God; they are the unbelievers, the atheists. *"To know God is to do justice."* Gustavo shows how this theme permeates the biblical story; encapsulated in this one passage, it appears everywhere. To know such a God is to do justice, which means siding with the oppressed, which means opposing the oppressors, which means involvement in conflict, which means "taking sides" in order to affirm rather than deny God. It is all of a piece.

How does Gustavo know? The Bible tells him so.

The Role of the Church

Biblical faith demands communal response. We can agree with Gustavo:

> To proclaim the Gospel . . . means to call people together in an "ecclesia", to unite them in an assembly. It is only in a community that faith can be lived in love; only there can it be celebrated and deepened; only there can it be lived in one single gesture, as fidelity to the Lord and solidarity with all people.[62]

But when he begins to describe the church, middle-class sensibilities begin to be tested. For if God sides with the poor, and if Jesus was incarnate as one of the poor, then his church will have poverty as a central feature.

> Another solid line of effort will be our commitment to a genuine poverty. . . . We must live in a Church that is not only open to the poor but poor itself.[63]

> If the Church wants to be faithful to the God of Jesus Christ, it has to rethink itself *from below*, from the position of the poor of this world, the exploited classes, the despised races, the marginal cultures. It must descend into the world's hells and commune with poverty, injustice, the struggles and hopes of the dispossessed because of them is the Kingdom of Heaven. Basically it means the Church living as a Church the way many of its own members live as human beings. Being reborn as a Church means dying to a history of oppression and complicity. Its power to live anew depends on whether it has the courage to die. This is its passover.[64]

This will be costly. Once again, to be *for* the poor, is to be *against* those who keep them poor. But that means a break with the established order. To establish real solidarity with oppressed people, then the first step is for the Church as a whole to break its many ties with the present order . . . accepting the fact that the future cast of the Church will be radically different from the one we know today. It will mean incurring the wrath of the groups in power—with all the risks that entails. Above all, it will mean believing in the revolutionary and liberating power of the gospel, i.e. believing in the Lord . . .[65]

In the language of Latin America, the church will become the "popular church." To us, such a phrase suggests that the church should take "popular" stands, go along with the *status quo*, and refuse to ruffle beards. But in Latin America it means just the opposite: a "popular" church will be a grassroots church, a church "from below" and therefore a militant church, a new and powerful "sign of the Kingdom."

A Church which is born from the people, from a people who rip the Gospel from the hands of the powerful of this world, who impede its use as a justifying element for a situation which is contrary to the will of the liberating God.

. . . [who] expropriate the gospel from those who consider themselves its privileged owners. The gospel tells us that the sign that the kingdom has come is that the poor are evangelized.[66]

Here is Gustavo's view of what such a church would look like:

What is envisaged in this view is the creation of Christian communities in which the private owners of the goods of this world cease to be the masters of the Gospel; communities in which the dispossessed can bring about a social appropriation of the Gospel. Such groups would prophetically proclaim a Church wholly at the service of persons in their battle to be persons; a creative and critical service always, because rooted in the Gospel. This struggle for full personhood follows a way difficult to understand from the old world in which the Word has been and still is lived, thought and proclaimed. Only by putting down roots among the marginated, exploited persons and rising from among these persons themselves, from their aspirations, interests, struggles, cultural categories, will a people of God be forged which will be a Church of the people, which will cause *all* persons to listen to the gospel message and will be a sign of the liberation of the Lord of history.[67]

"Faith and Works" and "Spirituality"

Faith is the fruit of deeds, and deeds are the seedbed of faith, but there is a circularity here that is never fully overcome.

> Christ came to establish not bondage but liberation from bondage. The core of his message is the Father's saving and liberative love. It must also be the core of our Christian life and our theology.[68]

Our response to the claims of faith is not intellection but action:

> The God who liberates in history, the Christ made poor, can only be preached with works, with gestures in a practice of solidarity with the poor.[69]

For Gustavo, as for all Christians, there is a dialectic between faith and works. There is also a clear priority:

> In the act of doing, our faith is made truth, not only for others but for ourselves as well. . . . Without action the word is susceptible to many interpretations. Moreover, saying what one lives and does leads to a more conscious and profound living and doing of what one expresses.
>
> However, the relation between act and word is asymmetrical: *the act is what fundamentally counts.*[70]

So there is a real place for "spirituality" in liberation. In conversation, confronted with charges that liberation theology neglects this dimension, Gustavo energetically responds, "Spirituality?. . . Is a good word." More formally:

> An authentic and profound sense of God does not preclude awareness of the poor and the questions they raise. "Spirituality" does not preclude "social conscience." The real incompatibility is between bourgeois individualism and spirituality.[71]

Gustavo wants to make sure that spirituality, rather than representing a retreat from the world of the oppressed, becomes a galvanizing force within it. Its importance for him is symbolized by the fact that one of the crucial sections of *A Theology of Liberation* is entitled "A Spirituality of Liberation" (pp. 203–208).

> Any attempt to separate the love of God from the love of our neighbor gives rise to attitudes which impoverish the one or

the other. It is easy to set a "praxis of heaven" against a "praxis of earth" . . . easy, but not in accord with the Gospel.[72]

A volume that Gustavo edited with Claude Geffré (and containing one of his best discussions of spirituality) is entitled *The Mystical and Political Dimension of the Christian Faith*. Two things are noteworthy about the title: (a) "mystical" and "political" are conjoined, not separated; and (b) their conjoining is described as a single "dimension," not as separate "dimensions."

Because there is only a single dimension, there is always hope, no matter how bleak things may look. The Christian dimension always includes hope—an appropriate note on which to conclude a closer look at the second act:

> The times which are being lived through in Latin America do not allow of any euphoria. The spirituality of the Exodus is no less important than that of the Exile. The joy of the Resurrection requires first death on the Cross—and this can take differing forms. But hope is always there. The situation which is being lived in the continent perhaps makes us live and understand in a renewed form what Paul called "to hope against all hope."[73]

CHAPTER SIX

The Critics Weigh In, Briefly

weigh in (vi) 1: to have oneself or one's possession (as baggage) weighed, *esp*: to have oneself weighed in connection with an athletic contest 2: to enter as a participant.
—*Webster's New Collegiate Dictionary*, p. 1328

After the opening night at a play, the critics take over. Sometimes they agree that the play is a triumph, or, conversely, that it is a dud. More often the reviews are "mixed"; some critics like it, some do not, the rest are not sure. Since their diverse judgments are all reactions to the same performance and script, we often learn more about the reviewers than about the play itself. Their judgment, critical ability, intuition and taste are likewise on trial.

When contestants "weigh in" before an athletic contest, they make themselves accountable to certain criteria, and the determination of whether they are eligible or disqualified is made by others. As Webster's second definition indicates, they become participants in a struggle.

The same thing is true of the critics of Gustavo's theology. They, too, "weigh in" as participants in a struggle. They are no longer spectators. They take sides, and the nature of their critique demonstrates which side they are on.

After reading many critics of Gustavo's theology, I have come to the conclusion that when most of them weigh in, they are found wanting. If Gustavo is to be held accountable by the critics, the critics can also be held accountable by Gustavo.

That they have failed to do him justice can be demonstrated by itemizing the stock-in-trade critiques one encounters with wearisome frequency: Gustavo's theology is "mere horizontalism," lacking the vertical dimension of transcendence (variant: it is "mere reductionism" or "mere" almost anything else); it is only a front for "Marxist ideology"; it fails to deal with the "spiritual dimension" of life; it advocates and "glorifies" violence; it fails to listen to the full biblical message; it attempts to capitalize on the latest theological "fad"; it is "elitist" (mutually exclusive variant: it reflects only what "the people" are thinking); it demands that the church become involved in a "purely political struggle"; it succumbs to "cultural relativism" and is conditioned by its point of origin (mutually exclusive variant: it is merely an imitation of European "political theology"); it is not "real" theology but only moral exhortation.

I would contend that the inaccuracy of these charges has been demonstrated by the exposition of Gustavo's thought in the previous five chapters; that such a judgment will be further reinforced by comments in the next chapter and the conclusion; and that those who want their liberation theology straight, and not diluted by interpreters, will find that ongoing exposure to Gustavo's own writings will dispose of the need to take such criticisms seriously. (Those who want further documentation can look at Chapter 4 of my *Theology in a New Key*, where I have examined in detail eight types of criticism of liberation theology.)

But there is a different kind of critique we must examine, which, although it originates in Latin America, has implications for us as well. Most Latin American critics assume that liberation theology is here to stay (however much they may deplore that fact) and so they seek to deal with it by *co-option*. They announce that they, too, are for liberation theology, only they want an "authentic" or "full" liberation theology. By this they mean a theology that gives *more* attention to the personal or "spiritual" liberation that Gustavo presumably overlooks. But they also mean a theology that gives *less* attention to the political-social-economic dimensions of life that Gustavo presumably overemphasizes.

In so doing, these critics deal with the terms "political" and "spiritual" in such a way that the former collapses into the latter, with the result that all that is really needed is "spiritual libera- tion." And since we *all* need "spiritual liberation"—whether we are rich or poor—distinctions between rich and poor, oppressors and oppressed, are likewise collapsed, and the need for structural change evaporates; the *status quo* will do just fine.

Such critics also fear what Gustavo's theology would do *to the life of the church*. Clearly, the traditional way of doing theology ("truths" handed down from above) is challenged when truth is held to emerge out of engagement in struggle. More important than that, the whole hierarchical structure needs radical re-defi- nition if the *communidades de base* (with which Gustavo is so closely associated) are to be the sources of ecclesiastical reflection and action; under the new arrangement, bishops would be expected to listen to the people, a reversal of the old-fashioned way, when the people were supposed to listen to the bishops. Most important of all, the necessity for the church to make "a preferential option for the poor" challenges all the church's traditional and historical alliances with the well-to-do. So Gustavo is criticized for insisting that "the church should take sides," it being assumed by the crit- ics that the church has never "taken sides" before. We have al- ready noted Gustavo's devastating response to the charge: the church has always "taken sides," almost invariably with the rich. What is needed now is for the church to "change sides," switching its allegiance from a subtle but thorough-going option for the rich and the *status quo*, to an overt and equally thorough-going option for the poor and the need for radical change on their be- half.

Here is where the presuppositions of such critics become transparent. Their real fear is not "political involvement" but rather "political involvement *on the left*," which is the only kind of political involvement today that can indicate a stand both for and with the poor. The quasi-paranoia about "Marxist influence" on Gustavo's theology is only the surface manifestation of a deeper fear, common to critics of almost every stripe: *radical change will result if Gustavo's theology is taken seriously.* When that issue is joined, of course, Gustavo has the Bible on his side. Which makes it a very one-sided match.

Let it be said for the critics that they have hit one theological nail squarely on the head. They are absolutely right that "radical change will result if Gustavo's theology is taken seriously." It will. The important thing theologically is not to understand the world but to change it.

Whether that is good news or bad depends on who is talking.

CHAPTER SEVEN

Getting on Stage:
The Importance of
Liberation Theology for Us

Commitment to the process of liberation introduces
Christians into a world quite unfamiliar to them and forces
them to make what we have called a qualitative leap—the
radical challenging of a social order and of its ideology and
the breaking with old ways of knowing.[74]

Rediscovering the others means entering their own world.
It also means a break with ours.

. . . It also means understanding that we cannot be *for* the
poor and oppressed if we are not *against* all that gives rise
to the exploitation of human beings.[75]

The first thing we ask Christians in the developed world is
that they influence the policies of their own countries.[76]

Avoiding the Question

We can avoid the challenge of liberation theology by reducing
it to a regional variant of "true" theology (i.e. ours), conceding
that it "says something to those people down there," but has nothing to say to us. Consequently, it is enough to study liberation
theology as a "significant trend," soon to be replaced by another
"significant trend," which we will also study. We can even write
and read small paperbacks about liberation theology's leading articulators.

We can also avoid the challenge of liberation theology by co-
opting it. We have seen how this happens in Latin America, but
Gustavo, aware that this can also be done in the U.S. and Europe
by ostensible friends, warns against attempts "to speak of the
same old things while simply adding the adjective 'liberating'

and, thereby, selling old merchandise which was beginning to pile up."[77] When the claims of liberation theology seem "obvious" to us, or just a restatement of "what we have always believed," or without real challenge, we can be sure that co-optation is well advanced.

Suppose we are determined to avoid such evasion tactics. What then?

The Impossibility of Neutrality; or, the Necessity of Taking Sides

If one thing is clear in Gustavo's theology it is that the privilege of neutrality is denied us. More strongly: the *illusion* of neutrality is denied us; those who claim neutrality have already given their vote to those in power. More strongly yet: it is not enough only to be *for* the oppressed, we must also be *against* the oppressors, even when they turn out to be not just a few evil people elsewhere, but great numbers of well-fed, well-clothed, well-intentioned people close to home—people like (and including) us.

At this point, many of us want to terminate the discussion; it has turned into a polemic, the analysis is unfair, the argument is loaded, the facts will not support it. At best, we want to suspend judgment until there is "a fuller analysis." Naturally, the fuller the analysis the better, but there is a very strong tendency to let the plea for fuller analysis become an eternal refuge from confronting the problem. When people say, "We are hurting . . . " we have an obligation to listen to them and rectify the situation causing the hurt. When people also say, " . . . and you are the ones who are hurting us," the obligation to listen is intensified, as is the need to rectify. Before we dismiss the complaint as outrageous, we must take seriously the possibility of its accuracy. The cries of the hurting always have an initial presumption of truth behind them.

Re-reading and Re-doing

How do we move from the illusion of neutrality to the reality of partisanship? There are at least two components: we are called to engage in *a new kind of analysis* and commit ourselves to *a new kind of action*. Put another way, we must engage in a *re-reading* of our situation (re-reading our history, our Bibles, our tradition) and a *re-doing* within that situation (involving a more radical kind of action than we engaged in before).

With which do we start? Our "Western" tradition stresses the priority of analysis: first find out what is going on, then act. Liberation theology tends to give a different message: you are already acting; out of your present commitment, analyze afresh what is going on, and then re-direct your action.

Actually, both analysis and action presuppose one another— there is no analysis totally uninfluenced by the context of the analyst, and there is no action totally uninformed by analysis. *Our* response to liberation theology, however, is more likely to be informed by a new analysis provided by someone else, than by self-threatening actions we initiate. So let us look first at the analysis.

The new kind of analysis is made from what Gustavo calls "the underside of history," and it involves seeing the world in a new way, i.e. from the perspective of the oppressed. This is not just an interesting exercise in empathy, because it forces us to confront the fact that outrageous conditions among the poor are caused by outrageous actions of the non-poor; the poor are poor because the rich are rich, and the rich are rich because they exploit the poor, and the rich want to stay rich badly enough to keep on exploiting the poor.

This is a "new kind of analysis," all right, and not a very comforting one. Let us try another example. The evil that leads to such a situation is not the fault of a few individuals or even a lot of individuals (though that can help); it is the fault of the entire system in which those individuals operate—a system in which the few benefit in handsome fashion while the many are exploited in ugly fashion. In this analysis, evil is "systemic," or "structural," suggesting that the sickness of our society is much more deep-seated than we had thought, and suggesting the even more drastic thought that a drastic illness may call for drastic surgery.

We also confront a new kind of analysis in looking at human rights. We tend to stress *individual* human rights—the right to protest, to express minority opinions, to be answerable to ourselves alone, so long as we do not violate the rights of others. But the counter analysis, while not down-grading such rights, lays greater stress on *social* human rights—the right of all people to jobs, housing, food, medical care, education. These are the rights "the wretched of the earth" truly need. Human rights in Latin America will not have been won when it can be announced that no more political prisoners are undergoing torture. They will have been won only when it can be announced that there are jobs for all, food for all, medical facilities for all, and so on.

How does one move from "a new kind of analysis" to "a new kind of action"? There is only one way: through involvement in the struggle of those who see the world in such a fashion. Gustavo cites a lesson from Bartolomé de Las Casas:

> Participation in a concrete historical process—such as the lives of the oppressed—enables one to perceive aspects of the Christian message that theorizing fails to reveal.[78]

The analysis cannot be *our* analysis so long as it proceeds in a vacuum. *It must be validated by engagement.*

Engagement is the hard part. Hearing an analysis is easy, if devastating. But engagement involves change and risk, two of the things we fear most. For most of us it involves changing sides, expending our efforts on behalf of the dispossessed, when our previous efforts have been expended on behalf of the well-to-do, whose major fear is always that the dispossessed might gain power.

Changing sides does not mean going to Latin America and stirring up a revolution (from which we can always disengage and come back home). It does mean finding those places where our national power is working destructively, and working within our own situation to re-direct the use of that power. The United States, for example, supported the brutal Somoza regime in Nicaragua for forty years, underwriting and sponsoring injustice. The

Pentagon, the State Department, the business community, the CIA, always found ways to "justify" that support. Perhaps we could learn from that tragic example how to avoid repeating the error elsewhere. Gustavo has some down-to-earth advice about how we can influence policy:

> The first thing is to become informed about what is happening in Latin America, and about the participation of the U.S. government and U.S. companies in Latin American affairs, and denounce this. Afterward, have as a criterion for domestic political action this intervention of the U.S. government and private companies. This should provide a criterion for political action in deciding which candidates to support.[79]

Recognizing the Radical Nature of the Demand

The cost of all this would be high. It would mean becoming "betrayers of our class," taking strong issue with the assumptions, norms, and values of the society that supports us, feeds us, and pays us. It would mean breaking with the convictions of many of our friends and most of our society. For, as Gustavo himself points out, "We cannot be *for* the poor and oppressed if we are not *against* all that gives rise to the exploitation of human beings."[80] Jürgen Moltmann, no "liberation theologian," has grasped what this means: "Whoever wants genuine communion with the victims must become the enemy of their enemies . . . To be free from the oppressive prison of one's society means to become a 'stranger among one's own people.'"[81]

So the impact of liberation theology is threatening and costly. And yet there is not a statement in the previous paragraph that would not have been true of Christians in the first century. This is not a new bind for twentieth century Christians, in other words; it has been the nature of the case since Christianity's inception.

An example of our evasion of this truth is the consistent way "Western" exegetes have de-fused the radical demand that Jesus made upon the Rich Young Ruler who had "great possessions." Jesus' statement is uncompromising; it is not enough to have followed the commandments from our youth; one thing is still lacking—selling all that we have, giving to the poor, and then following Jesus.

It is part of my own theological confusion (or timidity) that I am not sure just how we rich young (and old) rulers of the twentieth century put that demand into practice today, but I am sure that the demand is there and that the promise of the gospel will be found only on the far side of the demand.

Here Gustavo has a special word for the theologians. He points out that in his part of the world doing theology may mean prison, torture and death, for the tyrants have learned that theology and Christian commitment are their enemies. This is naturally cause for concern, but it is also a source of hope:

> If we are not able to speak about the real deaths of our people today we will not be able to speak about life and resurrection; we will not understand today what the Lord's resurrection means.[82]

The route to resurrection goes through death. That is a condition laid on Christians that mirrors what happened when God embraced the full conditions of humanity.

But there is a second kind of death as well, which Gustavo calls the death of "the intelligence of the intelligent; it is the death of the theologian as an intellectual."[83]

Now *there* is a death that strikes close to the bone of theologians . . . the death of theological "systems," the death of privileged positions, the death of any intellectual inside track. This is madness. Not a madness Gustavo generated, not even a madness Paul created, though a madness on which Paul reports. And Gustavo stands well within the Pauline tradition when he says, "The madness of the cross is the madness of the intelligence of the intelligent. It really is madness; it is death for this type of intelligence."[84]

So not even theologians are exempted from risk. Indeed, their jeopardy is double: physical death and/or intellectual death, death to all they have held dear, so that out of their death the new may come.

It sounds exactly like the New Testament.

Liberation Theology and the Church

All of this is stern stuff. (Death is particularly stern stuff.) Individuals do not easily rise to such heights. But sometimes groups can sustain individuals, or act corporately in ways individuals cannot. So let us examine what might begin to happen if we took liberation theology seriously in the church.

1. We would first of all *listen*. We would try to understand how we are perceived by others, even though the portrait is not flattering. We would listen to how the others deal with Scripture, even though what they hear threatens us. We would be open to new analyses of how power works in the world, even though the analyses suggest that we have too much. And we would also take heart that there is a community within which hard words can be spoken and heard in love.

2. We would realize that churches, like individuals, must *change sides*. Some, in Latin America, have already done that. What would it mean for *us* to change sides and make a "preferential option for the poor"? Initially, it would mean giving increasing voice (and authority) to minority groups who have been ecclesiastically disenfranchised in the past—blacks, Hispanics, women, homosexuals, and many more. And since such things are not likely to happen widely within our establishment structures, we would need a third ingredient.

3. We would create our own version of *communidades de base*, small groups of Christians who still affiliate with an overall structure, but also meet for reflection and action in small, intentional groups committed to "changing sides" and already trying to do so. Such groups would not only try to be living examples of their own convictions, but also try to exert creative pressures on their denominational structures for greater venturesomeness on behalf of the oppressed.

4. We would enter unashamedly into the *political arena*, since that is where decisions are made that affect the dispossessed, but we would also try to be more effective watchdogs in the *economic arena*, where the power in our society is increasingly located. For individuals, this would mean serious exploration of how a social-

ist option could be implemented in a culture frightened to death of the word, let alone the reality. For churches, it would mean giving support to the right of individuals to explore the option, report on it, try it.

5. As a way of moving in the above directions, we would see the church as *the global community*, rather than the national, "class," or denominational community. Such a vision would provide the base from which to attack the policies of any nation (not least our own) that were designed to shore up one nation at the cost of exploitation of other nations. It would also provide a base of *solidarity* with those of other races, cultures and geographical locations, in working together on behalf of a gospel that has the power to transform the lives of all, in the direction of greater justice and love.

Liberation for Us; from Bad News to Good News

The bad news is clear: we are on the wrong side, we serve in Pharaoh's court, we enjoy benefits that are procured at crushing cost to others, we are complicit in oppression even if we are not active oppressors ourselves.

Such an indictment, by itself, can only fill us with guilt (or outrage) and immobilize us. But there is good news beyond the bad news; it is that we need not be oppressors, and that we can be liberated from an oppressor role that destroys us as well as those we try to dominate. The longer we maintain an oppressor role, or are simply the beneficiaries of a system that plays an oppressor role, the more locked in we become to keeping it that way. We become beholden to whatever the system demands of us, whether it be militant anti-socialism, inordinate tax dollars for "defense," or simply paranoid fear of all change. So our liberation is bound up with the liberation of the very people we fear. As long as we keep them in chains, we are in chains too. To be sure, our chains are a good deal more comfortable than theirs—so comfortable, in fact, that we are willing to pay the price of conformism and nationalistic chauvinism to keep ourselves so pleasantly fettered.

As Paulo Freire has pointed out, *those who dehumanize others dehumanize themselves*. So any struggle that helps the dehumanized victims become human again by freeing them, is a struggle that helps to humanize those who have oppressed them. Victories of "peoples' movements," the downfall of oppressors anywhere (often supported by Western governments) are blows for freedom, not only for them but ultimately for us, hard though that may initially be for us to believe. The battle lines in the struggle for liberation will vary in different places—economic exploitation, sexism, racism, political tyranny, on-the-job-conformism—but they are all part of the same struggle. North American and European whites do not have to work at cross purposes with North American and European blacks or Asians or South American Hispanics. The liberation of the latter will initially threaten the former, but finally it will be the condition of their liberation too.

The message of the gospel in the face of all this is that deliverance is possible from the worship of false gods, for the sake of worship of the true God. Only the true God can command the kind of allegiance that will liberate us *from* the need to be craven before the gods of our society—upward mobility, financial success, narrow nationalism, approval from our peers, and all the rest—and liberate us *for* empowerment by the God who frees us to work for a world based on justice, in which the necessities of the poor count for more than the luxuries of the rich. We too need the three kinds of liberation of which Gustavo speaks: liberation from oppressive systems, liberation from the notion that we are powerless to bring about change, and liberation from the sin that dominates our lives. Every time this begins to happen, new doors open.

Our Own Theology, Not an Import

Whatever liberation theology we develop must finally be our own, not Gustavo's transferred up here. We can, of course, learn from him. But ours must have its own focus: instead of dealing with the rights of *mestizos* we will deal with the rights of Native Americans; instead of relying on Mariátegui we will cite Frederick Douglass or Walter Rauschenbusch; instead of invoking the writings of Arguedas we will ask what it means to promise "liberty and justice *for all*." We will draw on our own heritage at its best, to remind us of its present shortcomings and to suggest new directions.

But it will also be a theology listening to and taking account of the affirmations of others—as we have tried to do in the above pages—and seeing that policies in our Western countries may be supporting those who deny full freedom to *mestizos* in Peru.

Perhaps our greatest liberation would be *the ability to let go*, to let go not only of the false gods described above, but also to let go of the need to dominate, to be on top, to be "number one" (which is only another way to talk about letting go of false gods). We will need to take a lot of our cues from elsewhere, learning not to speak for others any more, but clearing the decks so that others can speak for themselves. Gustavo is right:

> We definitely will not have an authentic theology of liberation until the oppressed themselves can freely and creatively express themselves in society and among the people of God, until they are the artisans of their own liberation, until they account with their own values for that hope of total liberation which they bear within them.[85]

There Is No Conclusion: the Curtain Stays Up, the Play Goes On, and We Are on Stage

The mediation of the historical task of the creation of a new humanity assures that liberation from sin and communion with God in solidarity with all humanity—manifested in political liberation and enriched by its contributions—does not fall into idealism and evasion. But, at the same time, this mediation prevents these manifestations from becoming translated into any kind of Christian ideology of political action or a politico-religious messianism. Christian hope opens us, in an attitude of spiritual childhood, to the gift of the future promised by God. It keeps us from any confusion of the Kingdom with any one historical stage, from any idolatry toward unavoidably ambiguous human achievement, from any absolutizing of revolution.[86]

With the exception of the quotation at the frontispiece of this book, the above paragraph may be the single most important thing we need to hear from Gustavo in conclusion. It is important first, because it reminds us of something important about *his* perspective (which the critics always ignore); and second, because it points to something important for *our* perspective (which we often ignore).

As far as *Gustavo's perspective* is concerned, it reminds us not only that he does not use the gospel to escape into "idealism or evasion" (temptations that would be totally out of character for him); but also that he does not use the gospel to escape into any of the following: (a) equating the gospel message with a specific "Christian ideology of political action," (b) identifying the gospel with a "political-religious messianism," (c) confusing the kingdom of God with some historical stage of human development, (d) developing idolatrous regard for ambiguous human achievements, or (e) absolutizing revolution as the fulness of the gospel (temptations that are also totally out of character for him, despite what the critics say).

That is quite a laundry list. It gives the lie once and for all to charges that Gustavo has "reduced" the gospel to "mere" human endeavor, or become idolatrously and uncritically committed to a single political option.

As far as *our perspective* is concerned, the paragraph is a continual *warning against complacency*, and that is perhaps the warning we most need to hear. Precisely because the gospel cannot be reduced to the kinds of equivalencies cited above, there is need for Christian vigilance on our part of a sort that well-fed Christians would usually like to avoid. Particularly when so much that we have held dear is already under fire, we would like to feel that retreat from the most egregious sins of complicity is enough, and that we thereby earn the right to be left alone, clutching whatever remaining comforts we have salvaged in the process. But if Gustavo is accused (wrongly) of trying to equate the gospel with an "absolutizing of revolution," we can be accused (rightly) of trying to equate the gospel with an "absolutizing of the *status quo*," or, at least, opting boldly for mere cosmetic improvement.

And those things liberation theology will never let us do. We, too, need to be reminded that the struggle on earth for a just society is never over. If full justice will never be achieved simply by a revolution of the left, it will even more assuredly never be achieved by the ongoing and unchallenged domination of the right. Furthermore, every advance, however secure it seems, is precarious, and can be neutralized or negated not only by naked power but (more likely) by that same evil power masquerading as good, and marching under such banners as "aid," "development," "moderation," "prudence," or "spiritual renewal."

One of our hymns begins, "The strife is o'er, the battle won." In heaven, perhaps; on earth, never. Never, as long as history lasts, will the script come to the last page, good emerge a permanent victor over evil, the *dénouement* arrive, the resolution be achieved, the curtain come down to a conclusion.

There is no conclusion. The curtain stays up and the play goes on.

And we are on stage.

Bibliographical Pointers

Liberation theology, still in its early stages, is not so much a hard-cover industry, as a constant exchange of mimeographed materials (often distributed clandestinely), notes, reports on conferences, essays and responses. A bibliography, to be faithful to such a subject matter, must reflect this variety of sources.

Gustavo's own writings are a bibliographer's nightmare. He quite justifiably uses similar lecture materials on different occasions in different parts of the world; one of these will be published in a given country and then a somewhat similar, but not quite identical, lecture will be published in another country. English translations of both articles will subsequently appear in the United States, and sometimes different translations of the same article will be published. The disentangling of all these sources makes the "synoptic problem" in New Testament scholarship seem like child's play.

Gustavo denies that he is a prolific author; confronted once with a sizeable bibliography of his writings in many languages, he looked at it and responded, "Is always the same article!" The disclaimer, although containing a grain of truth, is too modest; for one who leads an "activist" life at home and a teaching/lecturing life abroad, he has produced an extraordinary output. What follows is only a preliminary accounting.

Key Works in English

1. Books

Gustavo Gutiérrez and Richard Shaull. *Liberation and Change*. Edited by Ronald H. Stone. Atlanta: John Knox Press, 1977.

Gustavo Gutiérrez. *The Power of the Poor in History* (to be published by Orbis Books in 1981).

Praxis of Liberation and Christian Faith. San Antonio: Mexican American Cultural Center, 1974.

A Theology of Liberation: History, Politics, and Salvation. Edited and translated by Sister Caridad Inda and John Eagleson. Maryknoll: Orbis Books, 1973.

2. *Contributions to Books*

Gustavo Gutiérrez. "The Hope of Liberation." In *Mission Trends No. 3: Third World Theologies*, edited by Gerald H. Anderson and Thomas F. Stransky. New York and Grand Rapids: Paulist Press and Wm. B. Eerdmans Publishing Co., 1976.

"Introduction." In *Between Honesty and Hope*, edited by the Peruvian Bishops Commission for Social Action. Translated by John Drury. Maryknoll: Maryknoll Publications, 1970.

"A Latin American Perception of a Theology of Liberation." In *Conscientization for Liberation*, edited by Louis M. Colonnese. Washington, D.C.: United States Catholic Conference, 1971.

"Liberation Movements and Theology." In *Jesus Christ and Human Freedom*, edited by Edward Schillebeeckx and Bas Von Iersel. Concilium Series No. 93. New York: Herder and Herder, 1974.

"Liberation Praxis and Christian Faith." In *Frontiers of Theology in Latin America*, edited by Rosino Gibellini. Translated by John Drury. Maryknoll: Orbis Books, 1979.

"Liberation, Theology and Proclamation." In *The Mystical and Political Dimension of the Christian Faith*, edited by Claude Geffré and Gustavo Gutiérrez. Concilium Series No. 96. New York: Herder and Herder, 1974.

"The Poor in the Church." In *The Poor and the Church*, edited by Norbert Greinacher and Alois Müller. Concilium Series No. 104. New York: Seabury Books, 1977.

"Statement by Gustavo Gutiérrez." In *Theology in the Americas*, edited by Sergio Torres and John Eagleson. Maryknoll: Orbis Books, 1976.

"Theology and the Chinese Experience." In *Christianity and the New China*, Vol. II, edited by the U.S.A. National Committee for the World Lutheran Federation. South Pasadena: Ecclesia Productions, 1976.

"Two Theological Perspectives: Liberation Theology and Progressivist Theology." In *The Emergent Gospel: Theology from the Underside of History*, edited by Sergio Torres and Virginia Fabella. Maryknoll: Orbis Books, 1978.

"Voice of the Poor in the Church." In *Is Liberation Theology for North America?* New York: Theology in the Americas, 1978.

3. A Sampling of Articles

Gustavo Gutiérrez. "Faith and Freedom: Solidarity with the Alienated
and Confidence in the Future." *Horizon*, Spring 1975, pp. 25–60.

"Liberation and Development." *Cross Currents*, Summer 1971, pp.
243–56.

"Notes for a Theology of Liberation." *Theological Studies*
31(1970):243–61.

"The 'Preparatory Document' for Puebla: A Retreat from Commitment." *Christianity and Crisis*, 18 September 1979, pp. 211–18.

"Where Hunger Is, God Is Not." *The Witness'*, April 1977, pp.
4–7.

Key Works in Spanish

1. Books

Gustavo Gutiérrez. *La Fuerza Histórica de los Pobres: Selección de Trabajos*.
Lima: Centro de Estudios y Publicaciones (CEP), 1979. A collection
of essays, all but one written since *A Theology of Liberation*. To indicate the scope of the collection, the titles are here given in English:
Revelation and the Proclamation of God in History; Participating
in the Process of Liberation; Liberation Praxis and Christian Faith;
The Power of the Poor in History; The Preparatory Document for
Puebla; The Poor and Liberation at Puebla; Theology from the Underside of History; The Limits of Modern Theology; A Text of Bonhoeffer.

Líneas Pastorales de la Iglesia en América Latina. Segunda Edición.
Lima: CEP, 1968.

Teología de la liberación: perspectivas. Quinta Edición. Salamanca: Ediciones Sígueme, 1974.

Teología desde el reverso de la história. Lima: CEP, 1977.

2. Contributions to Books

Gustavo Gutiérrez. "Evagélio y Praxis de Liberación." In *Fe Cristiana y
Cambio Social en América Latina*, edited by Alvarez Alfonso. Salamanca: Ediciones Sígueme, 1973. (portions translated into English
in *Praxis of Liberation and Christian Faith* and in *Mission Trends
No. 3*.)

"Praxis de la Liberación, Teología y Evangelizacion." In *Liberación:
Diálogos en el CELAM*, edited by Consejo Episcopal Latinoameri-

cano. Bogotá: Secretariado General del CELAM, 1974. (portions translated into English in *The Mystical and Political Dimension of the Christian Faith*.)

Introductory essays to three volumes of source readings, all of which are included in *La Fuerza Histórica de los Pobres*, cited above. The volumes are:

Signos de Renovación. Lima: CEP, 1969. (English translation, *Between Honesty and Hope*.)

Signos de Liberación. Lima: CEP, 1973. (English translation of Gutiérrez' essay in *Frontiers of Latin American Theology*.)

Signos de Lucha y Esperanza. Lima: CEP, 1979.

3. Articles

The articles are too numerous for inclusion in a short bibliography. One, however, should be noted:

Gustavo Gutiérrez. "Bartolomé de las Casas: Libertád y liberación." *Paginas* Nos. 5–6 (1976): pp. 41–49. (English translation in *Liberation and Change*, pp. 60–68.)

Background Works

Richard J. Barnet and Ronald E. Muller. *Global Reach: The Power of Multinational Corporations*. New York: Simon and Schuster, 1974.

John Eagleson and Philip Scharper, editors. *Puebla and Beyond*. Maryknoll: Orbis Books, 1979.

Latin American Episcopal Council (CELAM). *The Church in the Present Day Transformation of Latin America in the Light of the Council*. Vol. II. Bogotá: General Secretariat of CELAM, 1970. (the report of the Medellín conference.)

José Míguez Bonino. *Doing Theology in a Revolutionary Situation*. Philadelphia: Fortress Press, 1975.

Roberto Oliveros. *Liberación y Teologiá: Génesis y Crecimiento de una Reflexión 1966–1976*. Lima: CEP, 1977.

Selected Works by Other Latin American Liberation Theologians

Leonardo Boff. *Liberating Grace*. Translated by John Drury. Maryknoll: Orbis Books, 1979.

Ernesto Cardenal, editor. *The Gospel in Solentame*. Four volumes. Translated by Donald D. Walsh. Maryknoll: Orbis Books, 1976–.

José Comblin. *The Church and the National Security State*. Maryknoll: Orbis Books, 1979.

Alejandro Cussianovich. *Religious Life and the Poor: Liberation Theology Perspectives*. Translated by John Drury. Maryknoll: Orbis Books, 1974.

José Porfirio Miranda. *Marx and the Bible: A Critique of the Philosophy of Oppression*. Translated by John Eagleson. Maryknoll: Orbis Books, 1974.

Juan Luis Segundo. *The Liberation of Theology*. Translated by John Drury. Maryknoll: Orbis Books, 1978.

Jon Sobrino. *Christology at the Crossroads*. Maryknoll: Orbis Books, 1978.

Notes

1. *The Militant Gospel*, trans. John Drury (Maryknoll: Orbis Books, 1977), p. 328.

2. *A Theology of Liberation: History, Politics, and Salvation*, eds. and trans. Sister Caridad Inda and John Eagleson (Maryknoll: Orbis Books, 1973), p. 308. Wording slightly altered.

3. "Editorial," in *The Mystical and Political Dimension of the Gospel*, eds. Claude Geffré and Gustavo Gutiérrez, Concilium Series No. 96 (New York: Herder and Herder, 1974), p. 11.

4. Gustavo Gutiérrez, "Two Theological Perspectives: Liberation Theology and Progressivist Theology," in *The Emergent Gospel*, eds. Sergio Torres and Virginia Fabella (Maryknoll: Orbis Books, 1978), p. 250.

5. For more on changing Catholic social perception in the 19th and 20th centuries see:

    Hugo Assman, *Theology for a Nomad Church* (Maryknoll: Orbis Books, 1976), especially Chapter 2.

    Hugo Latorre Cabal, *The Revolution of the Latin American Church* (Norman: University of Oklahoma Press, 1978).

    Enrique Dussel, *History and the Theology of Liberation* (Maryknoll: Orbis Books, 1976), especially Chapter 2.

6. Gutiérrez' introductions are included in *La Fuerza Histórica de Los Pobres*, soon to be available in English. The three volumes are entitled *Signos de Renovación* (1969), *Signos de Liberación* (1973), and *Signos de Lucha y Esperanza* (1979). The first is available in English as *Between Honesty and Hope*.

7. *Doing Theology in a Revolutionary Situation* (Philadelphia: Fortress Press, 1975), p. 157.

8. José Míguez Bonino, "Statement by José Míguez Bonino," in *Theology in the Americas*, eds. Sergio Torres and John Eagleson (Maryknoll: Orbis Books, 1976), p. 278, italics added.

9. Gutiérrez has written at length about Las Casas; the most convenient material in English is in *Liberation and Change*, pp. 60–68 (an article originally appearing in Spanish in *Paginas*), and *The Emergent Gospel*, pp. 242–245. The most accessible materials on Las Casas are:

> Juan Friede and Benjamin Keen, eds., *Bartolomé de las Casas in History* (DeKalb: Northern Illinois University Press, 1971).
> Lewis Hanke, *Aristotle and the American Indians* (Bloomington: Indiana University Press, 1959).
> Bartolomé de las Casas, *The Devastation of the Indies: A Brief Account* (New York: Seabury, 1974).

10. Gutiérrez, "Two Theological Perspectives," pp. 244–245.

11. "Terrorism, Liberation, and Sexuality," in *The Witness*, April 1977, p. 10.

12. Gutiérrez, "Two Theological Perspectives," p. 227.

13. Gustavo Gutiérrez, "The Poor in the Church," in *The Poor and the Church*, eds. Norbert Greinacher and Alois Müller, Concilium Series No. 104 (New York: Seabury Press, 1977), p. 15.

14. Gustavo Gutiérrez, "Introduction," in *Between Honesty and Hope*, Peruvian Bishops' Commission for Social Action, trans. John Drury (Maryknoll: Maryknoll Publications, 1970), p. xxi.

15. Gutiérrez, "Two Theological Perspectives," p. 243.

16. *Ibid.*, p. 240.

17. Cf. *Theology in the Americas*, p. 311.

18. Gustavo Gutiérrez and Richard Shaull, *Liberation and Change*, ed. Ronald H. Stone (Atlanta: John Knox Press, 1977), pp. 92–93.

19. Gustavo Gutiérrez, "Liberation, Theology and Proclamation," in *The Mystical and Political Dimension of the Gospel*, p. 60.

20. See the final chapter of *A Theology of Liberation*, "Poverty: Solidarity and Protest," pp. 287–306. The chapter can be understood independently, and should be read to supplement the brief exposition here.

21. Gutiérrez, *A Theology of Liberation*, p. 298.

22. Gutiérrez, "Two Theological Perspectives," p. 247.

23. *Ibid.*, p. 247.

24. Cf. the following for more information on the present situation in Latin and South America:

> José Comblin, *The Church and the National Security State* (Mary-knoll: Orbis Books, 1979).
>
> Penny Lernoux, *Cry of the People* (Garden City: Doubleday, 1980).
>
> José Míguez Bonino, *Doing Theology in a Revolutionary Situation* (Philadelphia: Fortress Press, 1975).
>
> G. MacEoin, *Revolution Next Door: Latin America in the 1970s* (New York: Holt, Rinehart, and Winston, 1971).
>
> Ivan Vallier, *Catholicism, Social Control, and Modernization in Latin America* (Englewood Cliffs: Prentice Hall, 1970).

25. Gutiérrez quoted in "Gustavo Gutiérrez," Agostin Bono, *National Catholic Reporter*, 15 February 1977, p. 17.

26. Gustavo Gutiérrez, "Where Hunger Is, God Is Not," *The Witness*, April 1977, p. 4.

27. Gutiérrez and Shaull, *Liberation and Change*, p. 77.

28. I have dealt with this matter in *Theology in a New Key* (Philadelphia: Westminster Press, 1979), pp. 110–113, and more fully in *Religion and Violence* (Philadelphia: Westminster, 1973), especially Chapters 3 and 4, to which the reader is referred for fuller elaboration.

29. "Terrorism, Liberation, and Sexuality," p. 10.

30. Bono, "Gustavo Gutiérrez," p. 17.

31. Gutiérrez, "The Poor in the Church," p. 15.

32. Gutiérrez and Shaull, *Liberation and Change*, p. 87.

33. Gustavo Gutiérrez, "The Hope of Liberation," in *Mission Trends No. 3: Third World Theologies*, eds. Gerald H. Anderson and Thomas F. Stransky (New York and Grand Rapids: Paulist Press and Wm. B. Eerdmans Publishing Co., 1976), p. 67.

34. Gutiérrez and Shaull, *Liberation and Change*, p. 89. Wording slightly altered.

35. Gutiérrez, "Two Theological Perspectives," p. 250.

36. Gutiérrez, *A Theology of Liberation*, p. 266.

37. In what follows, I am adapting portions of an unpublished lecture by Gutiérrez, called "Two Theological Perspectives," as well as ma-

terial from "Teología desda el reverso de la historia," in *La Fuerza Histórica de los Pobres*, soon to be available in English.

38. Gutiérrez' most extended treatments of Metz in English are in *A Theology of Liberation*, pp. 220–225, and in *Liberation and Change*, pp. 57–59.

39. Gutiérrez, *A Theology of Liberation*, p. 224. Wording slightly altered.

40. *Ibid.*, p. 224.

41. Gutiérrez, "Two Theological Perspectives," p. 237.

42. Gutiérrez, "The Poor in the Church," p. 14.

43. Gutiérrez, "Two Theological Perspectives," p. 249.

44. *Ibid.*, p. 234.

45. Gutiérrez, "The Poor in the Church," p. 12. Cf. also *Liberation and Change*, pp. 53–4.

46. Gutiérrez, "Liberation, Theology and Proclamation," p. 67.

47. *Ibid.*, p. 66. Wording slightly altered.

48. Gutiérrez and Shaull, *Liberation and Change*, p. 85.

49. *Ibid.*, p. 84.

50. Cf., most compactly, *A Theology of Liberation*, pp. 36–37, 176ff.

51. Gutiérrez, *A Theology of Liberation*, p. 37. Wording slightly altered.

52. "Terrorism, Liberation, and Sexuality," p. 10.

53. In "Revelación y Anuncio de Dios en la Historía," in *La Fuerza Histórica de los Pobres*. This essay alone is sufficient to lay to rest any charges that Gutiérrez' theology is not sufficiently "Christian." Cf. also *A Theology of Liberation*, "Christ and Complete Liberation," pp. 168–178.

54. Gutiérrez, *La Fuerza Histórica de Los Pobres*, p. 29, my translation.

55. Isaiah 32:17, cf. *A Theology of Liberation*, p. 168.

56. Gutiérrez, *A Theology of Liberation*, p. 167.

57. *Ibid.*, p. 168.

58. *Ibid.*, p. 168.

59. *Ibid.*, p. 238.

60. *Ibid.*, p. 273.

61. *Ibid.*, p. 276.

62. Gutiérrez, "Liberation, Theology and Proclamation," pp. 71–72. Wording slightly altered.

63. Gutiérrez, "Introduction," in *Between Honesty and Hope*, pp. xxii–xxiii.

64. Gutiérrez, "The Poor in the Church," p. 13.

65. Gutiérrez, "Introduction," in *Between Honesty and Hope*, p. xvii.

66. Gutiérrez and Shaull, *Liberation and Change*, p. 93.

67. Gutiérrez, "Liberation, Theology and Proclamation," p. 76. Wording slightly altered.

68. Gutiérrez, "Two Theological Perspectives," p. 27.

69. Gutiérrez and Shaull, *Liberation and Change*, p. 88.

70. *Ibid.*, italics added.

71. Gutiérrez, "Two Theological Perspectives," p. 251.

72. Gutiérrez, "Liberation, Theology and Proclamation," p. 63.

73. *Ibid.*, p. 77.

74. Gutiérrez, "The Hope of Liberation," p. 65.

75. Gutiérrez, "Liberation, Theology and Proclamation," pp. 59–60. Wording slightly altered.

76. Bono, "Gustavo Gutiérrez," p. 16.

77. Gutiérrez and Shaull, *Liberation and Change*, p. 86.

78. Gutiérrez, "Two Theological Perspectives," p. 244.

79. Bono, "Gustavo Gutiérrez," p. 16.

80. Gutiérrez, "Liberation, Theology and Proclamation," p. 60.

81. Jürgen Moltmann with Douglas Meeks, "The Liberation of Oppressors," *Christianity and Crisis*, 25 December 1978, p. 316.

82. Gustavo Gutiérrez, "The Voice of the Poor in the Church," in *Is Liberation Theology for North America*, ed. Theology in the Americas (New York, 1979), p. 32.

83. *Ibid.*, p. 31.

84. *Ibid.*, p. 31.

85. Gutiérrez, "The Hope of Liberation," p. 85.

86. Gutiérrez, *A Theology of Liberation*, p. 238.